Studies in social administration

General editor: Professor T. E. Chester, CBE

Financial help in social work

£ 1·56 N/H

Studies in social administration

Financial help in social work

A study of preventive work with families
under the Children and Young Persons Act, 1963

Jean S. Heywood and Barbara K. Allen

Manchester University Press

© 1971 Manchester University Press

Published by the University of Manchester at
The University Press
316–324 Oxford Road, Manchester M13 9NR

ISBN 0 7190 0487 X

Printed at the St Ann's Press, Park Road, Altrincham

Contents

Foreword

Chapter 1 describes how twenty-six local authorities in the Northwest and the Universities of Manchester and Liverpool came together to plan some research into current problems of common concern. This study of the way in which Section 1 of the Children and Young Persons Act, 1963, was being implemented was undertaken by the Department of Social Administration of Manchester University. We could not have done it without the most generous co-operation of many individual officers at all levels in the five children's departments concerned, whose policies and practices we were allowed to explore in depth. We were also encouraged and supported with the greatest patience by a steering committee, chaired by Alderman Mrs W. Kettle, JP, which met six times between 1966 and 1970 to arrange for the financing of the research and to keep the consortium of local authorities informed as to how the project was developing.

We had hoped that this study would have been completed earlier but, as so often happens, the collection, computation and analysis of the findings about the circumstances of the families helped, took longer than anticipated. Also the writing up of the four basic case studies and the checking of the facts and our interpretation of them with the children's departments concerned were held up by the illness of our research worker, Miss Barbara Allen, at a crucial stage. We were fortunate in that Dr Jean Heywood, who had been closely associated with the enterprise from the beginning, was able to take over the writing of the study for publication.

We all regret that it was not possible to include more of the detailed and interesting facts which our research worker and the child care officers discovered. Having decided to publish the study as a book, we wished to make sure that it would be widely read; books that are long and too statistical are not. We also wished to uncover and underline the long-term rather than the short-term determinants of social policy. Studies such as this are rarely justified in moving from the descriptive to the prescriptive. Wisdom prompts us to emphasise what are and what are likely to continue to be the important factors determining local policy in implementing legislation—particularly where the legislation sets only the broadest of aims and the most general indications as to how they are to be pursued.

Barbara N. Rodgers
Department of Social Administration
University of Manchester

July 1971

1. Family care and material aid in a children's department

The inauguration of local authority children's departments in 1948 highlighted the need for a family care service. In the absence of any residual public assistance service for families, the department which was set up to care for 'deprived' children became involved with the family problems lying behind the deprivation and began to build up a body of experience about them. Moreover, the perception that much of the residential provision available at the time did not meet the needs of children in care also led children's departments to seek to change their emphasis from the protection of deprived children to the prevention of deprivation.

The period of the early 'fifties was comparatively sound economically. The United Kingdom had, at one point, a balance of payments surplus, and the climate of thought which had consolidated the social service movement of 1948 was hopeful. Poverty was apparently diminishing, and was expected to diminish further. The only major piece of research into poverty undertaken since the war was that of Seebohm Rowntree and Lavers—*Poverty and the Welfare State*—which was published in 1951 and seemed to demonstrate forcibly the great improvement in living standards which had taken place since the 1930's. Only 1½ per cent of the survey population in York were now found to be living in poverty, compared with 18 per cent in a similar survey undertaken by Rowntree in York in 1936.[1]

In the same year the publication of John Bowlby's study *Maternal Care and Mental Health* stressed so dramatically the emotional needs of deprived children that workers were forced to concentrate more seriously on the quality of the relationships their service was providing. Their experience of the difficulties of substitute relationships caused them to emphasise the importance of

[1] The first disquieting study—Brian Able Smith and Peter Townsend, *The Poor and the Poorest*, was not made till 1965. The Child Poverty Action Group was formed the same year. For an account of the rediscovery of poverty see Ken Coates and Richard Silburn *Poverty: the Forgotten Englishmen*, a Penguin Special, 1970.

the child's natural family and the difficulty of finding adequate substitutes for it. In children's departments, many of whom were facing a rising child delinquency rate, a major social problem now seemed to be how one could most constructively work with a certain small group of very poor families who were unable to cope with the task of child-rearing. The Ingleby Committee was set up in 1956 to consider the problem. Their brief was to inquire into the working of the juvenile courts and also to examine 'whether local authorities responsible for child care under the Children Act 1948 in England and Wales should, taking into account action by voluntary organisations and the responsibilities of existing statutory services, be given new powers and duties to prevent or forestall the suffering of children through neglect in their own homes'. Influenced by the prevailing trends of thought, and under pressure from local authority representations and professional associations, in 1961 the Ingleby Committee reported, recommending that children's departments be given extended powers to promote the welfare of children and to work with families to prevent their break-down under stress and their consequent separation. The committee recommended that local authorities be enabled to spend money on such work with families, and these recommendations were embodied in the Children and Young Persons Act, 1963, in the following terms:

It shall be the duty of every local authority to make available such advice, guidance and assistance as may promote the welfare of children by diminishing the need to receive children into or keep them in care under the Children Act, 1948 . . . or to bring children before a juvenile court, and any provisions made by a local authority under this subsection may, if the local authority think fit, include provision for giving assistance in kind, or, in exceptional circumstances, in cash. [Section 1]

In order to fulfil their new duties most local authorities considerably increased the staff of their children's department, appointing social workers to work with families which still remained intact in the community. Our study is a description of the way in which four different local authorities gave assistance to those families in the terms of the Act, either in kind or in cash, and we have attempted to estimate the results of this assistance upon both the clients and their problems, and upon the work of the children's departments. Important in our study was our attempt to assess the way in which four different local authorities developed policies about the giving of financial and material aid (assistance in cash or kind). We have looked at the administration of these policies, and their interaction with the case work of the child care officers. The formation of policy is always a variable matter, influenced by a variety of different factors and attitudes, and we have tried to analyse some of these complexities.

The possibility of making official grants of money or goods at discretion was new to the personal social services. Previously such powers, carefully defined within a government code, had been exclusive to the National Assistance Board, which, in addition to weekly payments, could make grants for exceptional needs. Most voluntary social service organisations, of course, had a tradition of discretionary payment; they have usually inherited small private charitable bequests which are used to help clients in a crisis. Almost all medical social work departments in hospitals were operating similar small funds, known as 'Samaritan funds', as a legacy of their voluntary foundation. Education departments (particularly in the North) had often disbursed 'clog funds' to help poor children inadequately clothed, and the Education Act of 1944 gave powers to local education departments to make grants for shoes and clothing from official funds. Education departments vary in their use of these permissive powers, which are, however, usually administered on the basis of a fairly simple means test formula. Some few children's departments had also had access to small, circumscribed charitable funds (for example from mayors' charities and used for holidays for poor children), but there was no precedent, in the local authorities, for putting these new statutory powers into practice on a large scale, and the children's officers quickly became aware of the problems of discretion involved. But the same Children and Young Persons Act of 1963 which gave them power to assist in cash or kind gave power for the first time to local authorities to spend money on research into their child care problems, and considerable interest in research projects began to be expressed among the children's officers.[2]

The conference of the Children's Officers Association held at Oxford in October 1964 took research and the future as its main theme, and three research papers were given there which evoked

[2] The very first research project carried out by a local authority under this Act was the Preston Family Welfare Survey by Peter Wedge, and published by Preston borough in 1966.

considerable interest among the elected representatives who were present. Iris Goodacre gave an account of her survey of current adoption policy and practice, which included information about the three parties to adoption; Jean Packman analysed the size of the child care problem in the different, individual local authorities; and Roy Parker discussed research priorities in foster home care. Shortly afterwards, in November 1964, the North-west branch of the Association of Children's Officers held a one-day conference in Chester on research, with special reference to the powers given to local authorities to undertake research under Section 45 of the Children and Young Persons Act, 1963. Chairmen of children's committees and treasurers were invited to this conference and the importance of research in facilitating and clarifying the making of policy was emphasised.

Finally, representatives of the children's committees of the North-west region, children's officers, treasurers and local authority representatives met at Liverpool on 9 September 1965 to discuss the practical value of involving children's departments in a research project. A joint research committee was then formed to work with the two universities of Liverpool and Manchester on research projects which were felt to be needed to clarify problems in child care which the local authorities were experiencing. A series of meetings elucidated that the two difficulties upon which local authorities then most needed clarification were, first, their new powers to give material aid, and second, practices and policies relating to the short-term care of children.

The Manchester research was concerned with the first of these two projects. It was largely financed by the North-west local authorities, and in December 1966 the research worker, Miss Barbara Allen, was appointed. Miss Allen was a graduate in economics, politics and sociology and held the Home Office Letter of Recognition in Child Care. For the last four years she had worked in the children's department of a large Midland city and, at the time of her appointment, held the post of assistant area children's officer. Her brief was to 'explore the local authorities' experience in giving material aid under Section 1 of the 1963 Act, their original policies, the problems encountered and any emerging second thoughts'.

The representatives of Manchester University who undertook responsibility for directing the research expressed the hope that research would have a twofold value. First, it would be educative within the children's departments themselves, since the staff and committee would be able to share with each other their experiences in administering material assistance to families at risk, and in relating their own policies to the availability of material help from other local services. It was also hoped that the study might enable them to assess how effectively material assistance could be used in helping to solve the problems of families at risk, and how far their social work practice was being changed by their new powers to give material assistance.

The worker immediately began a pilot study in an area office of a children's department in a large county borough and, through a detailed questionnaire sent to all the local authorities in the North-west, obtained a general picture of the region to enable areas to be selected with interesting variations for the main study.

The North-west region is large and varied, consisting of two English counties, four Welsh counties, two large county boroughs (population over 500,000), seven medium-sized county boroughs and nine smaller county boroughs (population between 60,000 and 88,000). Variations are found not only in size and population range but in geographical structure, degree of industrialisation, economic resources, and culture. Some idea of the variety can be obtained by looking at the expenditure on financial assistance per thousand of the population under 16. We examined this for the census year 1966 and found a range between £18 per thousand children and £0·70.

Choosing the areas to study, therefore, required taking many factors into account when examining how the new powers were being used. First of all we needed to know what variations existed between children's departments, and to consider this we looked at certain factors relating to each local authority, using as sources of evidence the results of our own questionnaire and the annual returns produced by the Home Office.

The following factors were considered relevant to our study of financial and material aid, and they were used as a basis for selecting a variable and comparable group of local authorities for our research project:

1. The type of local authority (i.e. county borough, county council, rural or industrial area).

2. Population.
3. Expenditure in the form of financial assistance.
4. Expenditure on financial assistance per thousand of population and expenditure per thousand of population aged 0–16 inclusive.
5. The way in which financial assistance is given (e.g. by grants, loans or a guarantee scheme).
6. The form of material aid or assistance in kind.
7. The number of voluntary organisations active in the area.
8. The existence or non-existence of written criteria and guide lines about disbursing aid.
9. The amount of specialisation on preventive work within departments.
10. The degree of delegation of the power to give financial or material aid.

Looking at the information we had about these factors enabled us to make suggestions to the local authority representatives at the research committee meeting held in February 1968, and they confirmed at their meeting in October the same year that the authorities studied would be a Welsh county, an English county, an industrial county borough and a county borough outside the great industrial conurbation. Several other factors were operative in making the final choice, as it was felt right that the study should represent the different types of authority within the region and be a cross-section of urban and rural districts so that final conclusions would be of benefit to all types of authorities.

The particular English county was chosen because, contrary to the practice of most authorities, it had formal, written guide lines and had established formal criteria about the disbursing of material aid. It had no system of guaranteeing rent, but a considerable housing problem, since rehousing and eviction were not the direct responsibility of the county council but of a host of small borough and urban and rural district councils in whose areas the families at risk lived. It had established a practice of giving loans, but a limit was placed by the council on the amount of financial grant or loan which could be approved by any area committee. It employed no specialist workers in the preventive field. It was inclined to pursue voluntary sources of material help first. It was also an example of a large two-tier authority likely to be the pattern, so it was thought, of local government in the future.

It was considered desirable to take a Welsh county, with its different culture and population, but in administration there were interesting contrasts with the English county. The Welsh county had no guide lines, but had a similar problem in housing, had a rent guarantee scheme and gave only a few loans but spent most of its expenditure on rent and rates. It had a specialist worker for families at risk.

Of all the county boroughs, industrial Milltown was found to be somewhat atypical of the region, and we therefore considered that it might be useful to examine it in more detail. The department had undertaken preventive work without giving material aid since the early 'fifties and had no guide lines covering the new powers. It had specialist workers with large case loads. The town had no rent guarantee scheme at the beginning, gave very little in financial grants, and then usually only in the form of small loans rarely exceeding £1.

Thus the English county and Milltown had some similarities in their absence of rent guarantees at the beginning, in their policy of limited loans, and some contrasts in their appointment of specialist staff, and their formalising and absence of rules about disbursing aid.

Nordale, outside the main industrial conurbation, was chosen as the fourth area and the second medium-sized county borough. Like Milltown, it had a core of specialist staff but with small case loads to undertake preventive work. It was the only medium-sized county borough to start work under the Act with a housing sub-letting scheme. Its main item of expenditure, like the English and Welsh counties, was on rent and rates, and it ranked third in the twenty-five authorities in the North-west in the amount of assistance it gave per head of the population—contrasting with Milltown, which ranked twenty-fourth.

The methodology used in our study is described by the field research worker in Appendix 1.

2. Aid and discretion

As we have seen, the powers to grant financial and material aid at the discretion of the local authority children's department came into force before the country was fully aware of the extent of poverty,[1] and the widespread need for a national policy to tackle it was under-estimated and was not yet seen to be a matter for public concern. At the time of our survey, however, in 1968, Brian Abel Smith and Peter Townsend had published their study *The Poor and the Poorest* in 1965 and in the same year the Child Poverty Action Group had been formed.

In 1966 the government introduced the supplementary benefits scheme, in which emphasis was laid on the concept of benefit as of right. A distinctive feature of the new supplementary benefits, as of the old national assistance scheme, is its powers of discretion, which enable its officers to take into account, with some flexibility, the claims of individually different circumstances. But since 1966 the concept of right to benefit has tended to spill over from the clear entitlement to allowances at the scale rate to these discretionary additions and exceptional needs grants—even though a 'right' dependent on the exercise of discretion can never be of the same order as one arising out of a determination of need by the application of a standard formula.

Examples of such discretionary awards are for special diets in the case of certain illnesses; for extra fuel in the case of the old or the housebound or of damp housing; for laundry costs for the incontinent or for extra clothing needed because of heavy wear and tear arising from a disability; domestic help for people who cannot do their own housework; fares to visit a relative in hospital, and so on.

Exceptional needs arising on single occasions, as opposed to continuing expenses, are provided for by the exceptional needs grant. For example, clothing and footwear may be provided by an exceptional lump sum payment if a family without reserves of capital has been living at or below supplementary benefit levels for

[1] We are here using the term in its relative, not its absolute, sense.

some time and, say, a member is about to leave hospital after a long stay; where a family is rehoused by a local authority from furnished accommodation payments may be made for major items of bedding or household equipment; fares may be paid to send the children of sick parents to relatives or friends.

After 1963 it became increasingly important that the basis or purpose of the discretion exercised by the National Assistance Board (later the Supplementary Benefits Commission), and of that exercised by children's departments, should be clearly understood, since both were often to be involved at the same time with the same family. The distinction is a fine one, more easily understood in general terms than in application. The Supplementary Benefits Commission (SBC) must exercise its discretion in order to fulfil its primary purpose of *meeting financial need,* normally by ensuring that the family receives sufficient money to meet its requirements, which cannot in every case be standardised, because of special or exceptional circumstances. The children's department must exercise its discretion (to give material aid) in relation to its primary purpose of *increasing the family's ability to cope with its difficulties,* in order to prevent a functional breakdown or the development of some delinquency in response to stress. The support and treatment given by the children's department are what is meant by the term 'case work', and case work includes procuring material and financial help when needed as well as the affirming of a client's strengths and exploring and clarifying with him a way out of the problem. Generally in cases of financial need the child care workers would help the client to use the employment services or the social security benefits to which sick or unemployed clients are entitled. Only when financial assistance cannot be obtained from these sources does the discretionary power to give material aid given to children's departments under the Children and Young Persons Act, 1963, come into play. Circular 204/1963, a Home Office explanatory memorandum on the Act (see Appendix 2), spells this out in paragraph 10, which is headed 'Liaison with National Assistance Board':

It is not intended that the power to give material assistance under Section 1 of the Act should be used to provide an alternative to national assistance or a child care supplement to national assistance payments—continuing payments would in any event have to be taken into account as a resource by the Board in deciding the amount of a

B

regular national assistance grant. It will therefore be necessary for the authority to arrange for close liaison with the National Assistance Board to ensure that assistance, whether in kind or in cash, is not given in circumstances where it could more appropriately be given by the Board or where the result would be an unjustifiable duplication of expenditure from public funds. Except in cases of emergency where the assistance, if it is to serve any useful purpose, must be given at once, the Board should be consulted before any assistance in cash or in kind is given. Where the head of a household is in full-time employment, the Board's powers to give assistance are extremely limited, and in such cases there will ordinarily be no need for the authority to consult with the Board.

Although helpful, this still leaves plenty of room for argument as to whether in any specific set of circumstances a financial grant to a family 'could more appropriately be given by the Board', exercising its discretionary powers to meet special or exceptional *need,* or by the children's department to prevent family breakdown. Assuming the NAB–SBC has decided, as only it can, that it is not appropriate, then what further limits are set on the discretion of the children's department to give material aid?

As defined in the *Concise Oxford Dictionary,* discretion is the 'liberty of deciding as one thinks fit, absolutely or within limits'. What are the limits? In our context they are set by the law and the agencies' resources and policy. According to the law, assistance in kind may be given as part of the process of preventing both family breakdown and individual delinquency, and only exceptionally may cash grants be made for this purpose.[2] But law and individual discretion can never be wholly mutually exclusive. The discretion to use such grants or payments is called into play only when the child care officer has assessed the needs of the case and thinks it is necessary to make such a grant to achieve the goal of the law: keeping the family together, or restoring a child back to his own home, or preventing a delinquent crisis arising. Grants would therefore seem to be justified when tied to a specific set of difficulties which are leading to family breakdown or delinquency, and not comparable with the situations where the SBC allows discretionary grants, for in their case the outcome of the situation is not so specifically envisaged, and the grants are in the form of relief of financial need and are not for the prevention of specific situations of neglect or family failure.

[2] Section 1(i) of the Children and Young Persons Act, 1963.

Case work is individualised, and each family's circumstances and personalities are different, so that assessments of the need for discretion for each family are different too. It would therefore be inappropriate for case workers to depend upon inflexible rules defining the situations in which they should recommend material or financial aid with the object of preventing neglect or cruelty or family break-up, or in order to help restore a child from statutory care back to his family's care. The only possible method of work relies upon the workers' on-the-spot assessment, his skill in diagnosis—diagnosis of what the problem is all about; of how it has arisen; of what social, economic and psychological factors are prolonging it; of what is the capacity of the family to cope—and a creative assessment of what steps need to be taken to stop the problem developing into a complete family breakdown, or, if the child is already in care, into complete family separation. Thinking on these lines is part of the social worker's skill, for which he has spent a long time training; there are no rules of thumb to be applied (no considerations of 'eligibility' or 'determination of need'), though a body of knowledge may be built up from a history of successful and unsuccessful cases and some broad concept developed of the sort of case which responds to a particular sort of help—help, for example, such as financial grants, loans of money or guarantees of rent, or some form of material assistance.

In our study we found that most children's departments did not have firm ruling guide lines based either on dogma or on precedent. It was, in fact, left to the child care worker to diagnose in each case what kind of help was most appropriate, and each department was slowly and carefully developing a policy out of its experience. The reason given for this lack of direction by most departments was that rules and regulations tend to become rigid, and this prevents them from responding to the complexity and variation of the human problems they have to work with. However, we found that, although the child care workers did work on a diagnostic rather than on a directed basis, their power to disburse money on behalf of the department when they had made their diagnosis and decision was influenced by the policy and thinking which lay behind the entire work of the department.

The policy about spending money and giving aid was something arrived at between workers and committee members as a result of local experience of needs, or organisation and administration in other departments of the corporation, and in outside bodies, both statutory and voluntary. This co-operation and deliberation, which accepted that the children's department could not be an isolated agency but was very much a part of the local situation, variously influenced the way in which the workers evolved methods of exercising the powers they had acquired under the 1963 Act.

We found two basic and related approaches to the disbursement of financial aid under the 1963 Act. First, there is the case work approach, in which a professional diagnosis is made of the *need* for the grant in order to reach a specific goal. Second, there is the committee approach of laying down limits to the *amount* of grant and exercising an overall decision about the need for it, in the light of the worker's evidence. A good deal of the committee's work has been simple ratification of the worker's diagnosis, but the amounts of money which are spent are small. It is possible that a committee, becoming concerned at the amount of money which is being spent, would reconsider whether to allow child care workers to make grants at their own discretion, or whether to impose more formal rules and regulations specifying what sort of cases are appropriate for aid, and which are not. The crux of the whole matter is whether the grant made by the worker is regarded as a matter of administrative discretion or as part of a professionally skilled diagnosis which the committee respects.

This sort of difference in criteria may lie behind the reasons why committees have not, on the whole, formulated their policies rigidly about the granting of financial aid. A number of other factors may also be relevant.

Home Office circular 204, already referred to, which drew attention to the importance of approaching the National Assistance Board first if clients were in receipt of assistance, also drew attention to the availability of charitable funds as a source of help, and defined assistance in cash and kind. It is also more than probable that committees were reluctant to lay down guide lines because of their inexperience of giving financial aid and their uncertainty about whether it should be encouraged or discouraged. Many departments in 1963 were anxious lest the demand made on them might be excessive and envisaged people thronging to the office to ask for their gas, electricity or rent arrears to be paid. Therefore many departments were careful not to broadcast their new powers and informally emphasised that they could be used only in exceptional circumstances or within the framework of prevention or restoring a child to his home. Some departments, too, wished to experiment first, and preferred giving loans or guarantees to pay arrears where it seemed appropriate, rather than making actual cash grants. The newness of this whole field is reflected in the — original estimates set by departments, which were in the nature of inspired guesses and show great variations even between similar local authorities.

Lastly, financial aid is linked to the duty 'to make available such advice, guidance and assistance as may promote the welfare of children by diminishing the need to receive children into or keep them in care under the Children Act, 1948 . . . or bring children before a juvenile court'. The report of the Ingleby Committee (1961), which led to the inclusion of this duty in the 1963 Children and Young Persons Act, distinguished three stages in dealing with prevention:

(a) The detection of families at risk.
(b) The investigation and diagnosis of the particular problem.
(c) Treatment: the provision of facilities and services to meet the families' needs and to reduce the stresses and dangers that they face.

Decisions in these matters are clearly professional and diagnostic, and not a matter of administrative discretion. Departments do, however, differ greatly in their interpretation of the preventive emphasis of the Act, and these differences of policy create different situations where discretion has to be used. Some will consider assistance in kind or cash only when there is an *imminent* chance of a child coming into care; others will give such assistance when there is only a remote chance of a family breakdown. Different professional views may also be taken about the effect of evictions because the rent has not been paid. One department will argue that even if the family is given accommodation for homeless families this in itself will add to the strain and breakdown within the family and lead eventually to the admission of children into care. Therefore help with the payment of rent is permissible. Other departments hold that the provision of accommodation for homeless families solves the problem and removes the need for the children's department to intervene. Others still may regard eviction as a crisis situation which the family may have to face in order to learn about reality, and before case work with them can truly begin.

3. Discretion and diagnosis

We have seen the framework in which the child care worker generally operates—unable to give money without it being tied to the conditions of prevention of family breakdown or delinquency, and rehabilitation or restoration of the child to his own home. We have seen that the grants are, therefore, specifically 'goal-directed' —more than those of the Supplementary Benefits Commission are likely to be. One would expect formal directions, if they existed, to be concerned with the relation between the grant and the goal, and certainly the case work of the child care workers should give evidence of this. Since, however, most authorities do not have guide lines, let us look generally at the position of child care workers who must put up a 'good case' to obtain financial assistance for a client.

Knowing that their recommendation must go to a senior member of staff or before the committee, it is important for them to prepare the case well to reduce the possibility of refusal. Too many refusals could inhibit a child care officer from making future requests, and lead him to become uncertain about the purpose of help. In the absence of formal guide lines, therefore, a great deal of informal discussion about the case is likely at various levels, and agency policy must be explored and determined in the knowledge that precedents are being created on which future modifications of policy will be made. All this takes a great deal of time. It may well be that some child care officers find it easier to refer a family to another agency for financial aid, especially as approaching other agencies is encouraged by some departments. There are, however, certain informal factors operating within children's departments which may be just as effectively helpful to the worker as official guide lines.

First, there is the supervision and help of the experienced senior staff. Second, there are the periodic reviews which some departments undertake of preventive cases, which familiarise staff with the needs of families and their responses to differentiated help. These reviews of what is happening can help to identify cases where a worker hesitated to recommend the use of financial aid, or where it was given freely; results can then be considered and compared, and this enables some knowledge about practice to be accumulated. Third, there is the common denominator test applied by the fact that the children's officers or senior worker assesses cases in the light of the need for committee approval. Fourth, there is the approach of child care officers, whose training is aimed at examining the family's total situation and its needs, both emotional and environmental. This approach, as we have said, includes the use of financial aid along with other forms of help for the family. These four factors ensure that decisions about financial aid are never made in a vacuum.

However, the fact that aid is linked to a case work goal—prevention of family break-up, or family rehabilitation—could mean that only clients who will respond to case work help by learning to cope effectively on their own will be given financial aid. The 'right' to this kind of help could then be denied on grounds of non-co-operation with the worker. It is, of course, very doubtful if this was ever the intention behind the Children and Young Persons Act of 1963. The Act must be seen in its totality, and it was important in that it promoted, for the first time, the concept of the child's entitlement to good parenthood, an on-going process of family development in which complex relationships interact with economic opportunities and social conditions. Social workers and committees now know that there are parents who need continual psychological support through crisis after crisis if they are to maintain this development all the time the children are at home and dependent on them. We wonder how far it has been generally accepted that some of these families need constant financial support too. At local government level we enter here the province of policy decisions in which the committee needs to be involved. Have the committees, as the public's representatives, accepted the need of some clients for more long-term financial support than the social security system currently allows, and if so, is this sort of help really appropriate for the local authority to give? It is not uncommon to hear the view expressed by child care workers that it is no good paying a family's arrears of rent, even to stave off eviction, because they will be in exactly the same situation in a year's time. A child care worker may be tempted to exclude such clients from grants because they cannot rise to a committee's expectations that financial aid given now will prevent financial problems recurring. If the department decides not to give financial aid it is then left with two alternatives: either to close the case and let the family go into welfare accommodation for the homeless, or to keep the case open and go through the experience of eviction with the family, giving them generous case work support, hoping that the eviction does in fact help the family to face up to reality and gain strength from the experience of coping (with help) in a crisis. This latter approach, which some theorists[1] would advocate, implies that a sound and tested relationship already exists between case worker and family, and also that a child care worker has the time to support the family in this crisis at a very intensive level. Many children's departments, however, have problems of staff shortage, especially of trained staff,[2] and may excuse themselves by saying they have not the time to work at this level. Such crisis work can also demand a level of tolerance of anxiety in the worker for which training, and a certain amount of aptitude, are essential.

Our researcher found further examples of recurring need for financial aid among the group of families constantly falling into debt because their earned income was below subsistence level, i.e. below that basic level of living allowed for human needs by the Supplementary Benefits Commission. Family income supplements, of course, did not exist at the time of our survey and we have not, therefore, been able to take them into account, but some families would have continued to live below—though not so far below—subsistence level despite the proposed family income supplements. It is clearly recognised, however, that these problems call for national, rather than local, solutions, and underline the temporary and expedient nature of financial aid under the 1963 Act in such cases.

Local authority children's departments, feeling their way into a new dimension of social work, have been thinking in terms of case work diagnosis and of developing social policies. But they cannot and should not act independently from those other agencies in the community able to give financial assistance. Over the past few

[1] Notably the crisis theory of G. Caplan. See the article 'Crisis theory and possibilities of therapeutic intervention' by Sydney Brandon in the *British Journal of Psychiatry*, vol. 117, No. 541, December 1970.

[2] On 31 March 1970 whole-time field officers of the local authority child care services in England and Wales totalled 4,064, of whom 1,999 held a professional qualification (Hansard, written answers, 22 April 1971).

years there has been a great deal of activity between voluntary relief-giving agencies, children's departments and local supplementary benefit officers so that each could determine their own sphere in relation to the others. Despite increased communication and levels of understanding about each other's function, however, we found that there remained a great deal of misunderstanding about the use of discretion. For example, a children's department might ask the supplementary benefit officers to let them know their rules and regulations governing the use of discretion, but on the other hand should the SB officers, or indeed any other agency, ask the children's department in turn for *their* guide lines, they could be met with the answer that each case is determined on its merits within the framework of Section 1 of the 1963 Children and Young Persons Act. Confusion could then arise about which cases should be referred to children's departments, since we have seen that the Act is open to different approaches in policy and that the work is governed by a diagnostic process.

However, in 1970 the SBC published its *Supplementary Benefits Handbook,* laying down, for the public to see, its own guide lines as to how discretion will be exercised in given circumstances. Writing seven years after the introduction of the new powers of aid in children's departments, one paragraph, which deals with the provision of exceptional grants to cover debts and rent arrears, is significant enough to quote:

87. The payment of a weekly supplementary pension or allowance is intended to cover all normal requirements, including heating and rent, and it is left to the recipient to budget for these items, whether the payments are made at weekly or longer intervals, in the same way he would have to do when working. Where because of mis-spending or mismanagement fuel debts or rent arrears arise, there will be a need for advice to solve the budgeting problem. This may well be a situation calling for a professional skill of the social work services, and in these circumstances the Commission seek the co-operation of the organisations concerned so that the approach to the case may be co-ordinated in the light of all the services available. Where, as a very exceptional use of their powers, the Commission make or contribute to payments *they take steps to prevent a recurrence of the situation.* The arrangements made may well involve payment to third parties, or, where appropriate, payment in kind. [Our italics.]

The SBC is in a very different position from any other government body, as its main function is giving benefit in the form of money. It must not only be fair as well as human, it must be manifestly seen to be fair. An example of this need to combine fairness with discretion is seen later on in the handbook, where, in another paragraph, the difficult problem of maintenance of separated mothers and children is faced, the difficulty of exercising discretion when there can be different goals—reconciliation or separation.

161. The Commission recognises the importance of reconciliation to separated families, and that any action taken by its officers, including the payment of benefit, might help to widen the breach between husband and wife; equally, however, the Commission feel bound to avoid a situation in which financial pressure on the wife forces her to agree to a reconciliation on almost any terms the husband cares to make. In resolving the problems which arise local officers co-operate with other welfare agencies such as probation officers (in England and Wales) and marriage guidance counsellors. There is also co-operation with social workers concerned with illegitimate children.

It will be seen from these two quotations that there can be great confusion about the main areas of discretion of the SBC and the children's departments. When a family supervised by the children's department and receiving supplementary benefits gets into electricity or rent arrears, it is likely that the children's department will feel that this is clearly a case where the SB officers should pay an exceptional needs grant. However, the SB officers have to decide within their own frame of reference whether or not this is an exceptional need, and whether steps can be taken to prevent it recurring. Complications may arise for them where full benefits have been paid which are supposed to cover fuel and lighting, as well as other necessities. This means that the SB officers would, in effect, have to justify paying the bill twice. They also must consider whether their action would discourage the client from saving to pay future bills and encourage him to be less careful with electricity in the expectation that the next bill would be paid. They must consider how they can prevent the situation arising again. There is inevitably an element of social work diagnosis in dealing with such cases; as the SBC now recognises, 'welfare' is not peripheral to its primary function of providing financial assistance to meet requirement but an integral part of the job of 'getting the money right'. Paricularly is this so when it is a question of a discretionary allowance or exceptional needs grant. A professional training for all the visiting staff of the SBC is not practical nor appropriate; in-service training must somehow be developed to cope with this inescapable commitment. SB officers are always under considerable strain. Not only do they have to know the often changing rules and regulations of their own department, but they also have to acquire detailed knowledge of all the other social services to which they can refer families with more complex problems. Moreover, the demand on the SBC by the public has recently increased considerably. The average number of claims made personally at each local office in December 1957 was 590; in December 1965 it was 810; in December 1967 it was 1,490! In addition, like many children's departments, they are having to cope with a rapid expansion of staff and a constant staff turnover, giving rise to the problem of training new entrants.[3] For all these reasons—the different goals of the work, the different functions of the agencies, the different bases of training—there can be great confusion about the use of discretion on both sides, and often a guide line mentioned on either side will be assumed by the other to be a regulation. When we were asked to undertake our study there was clearly a need for a greater knowledge of each other's practices. Both departments had problems in the same field, problems of discretion, diagnosis and policy. It was out of these problems and the need for clarification that our research was born.[4] In fact, we looked at the tensions inherent in all social work, that is, between the different approaches required in guarding the public purse and encouraging self-reliance in the client (the claims of public accountabiliy) and in working within a distinct sub-culture in which often self-reliance, and also hope, are both absent. This tension, it seems to us, significantly highlights the need for clarity about the purpose of social work, and emphasises its involvement in social administration. Only so will it realise its full potential for contributing to social change and to the development of sound and imaginative social policies.

[3] The SBC is obviously very much aware of the problems that have arisen. Special welfare officers are now employed in each region to visit difficult cases and in 1968 a professional social worker was appointed to advise the commission on its 'welfare' functions. Its staff training centre also organises courses in human relations which cover the emotional problems of clients, deals with services which can give treatment and support, and teaches some knowledge about the professional social worker's approach and skills.

[4] The arguments in this chapter draw heavily on the ideas expressed in Barbara K. Allen, 'Administration of discretion', *Case Conference*, vol. 15, No. 2, June 1968; Olive Stevenson, 'Problems of individual need and fair shares for all', *Social Work Today*, vol. 1, No. 1, April 1970; *Supplementary Benefits Handbook*, HMSO, 1970.

4. Milltown

The way in which children's departments approached their new task after 1963 was influenced by the way in which they had carried out their work in the preceding years. Milltown, for example, had built up a family care section specifically to undertake preventive work, although it had no powers to spend money, and had been accustomed, because it began as a pioneer experiment in the 1950's and because it was not a wealthy authority, to financial stringency. The department's experience of preventive work on a limited budget, and its realistic fears of demand for financial help exceeding supply, conditioned its policy after 1963. It did not broadcast its new powers. The majority of families in the sample were found to have debts on referral to the department. But the practice of the department after 1963 was based upon its earlier experience of working with families in poverty and its belief that giving financial aid was not compatible with case work help. Moreover, part of Milltown's cultural pattern was that of small, local, closely-knit factory communities which helped each other by lending in times of need, and the staff of the family care section had been in the habit of themselves giving small personal loans to clients in need.

Staff and committee now discussed their previous practice thoroughly and decided to continue it on an official basis. An annual estimate of expenditure was made for £50, an amount deliberately kept small because so many families were known to be in financial difficulties, and it was feared that the department would be overwhelmed with requests. At the time of our study the position was described in the following terms:

It is felt that case work and the distribution of large-scale material aid do not mix very easily and that the family care work of the department could become seriously distorted if the public came to see the department as a regular source of financial assistance. In a small, closely-knit area like a county borough, good news spreads fast and there would probably be a rapid build-up of pressure to provide ever-increasing amounts of such assistance. It is fatally easy for officers, both in the department and outside it, to find a temporary solution to a problem in terms of money, which is neither constructive nor lasting. The demerits are that children have occasionally been received into care because their parents were evicted for non-payment of rent or sent to prison for non-payment of fines, etc. [Department's reply to questionnaire, summer 1967.]

It was therefore decided that small loans of up to £2, which must be repaid, could be given in emergencies. Individual officers could spend up to £2 under the supervision of the principal family care officer, and over £2 with the approval of the children's officer. In the past the tradition of personal relationships between officers and clients had meant that the loans were almost invariably repaid.

When we chose to study Milltown it had no scheme of rent guarantees, and no financial aid beyond loans was being given. Payment of clients' debts in the form of gas and electricity bills was not a part of its practice. In 1967 Milltown began to evolve a rent indemnity scheme for a number of reasons, among them the fact that its cautious approach towards financial aid had had certain repercussions. One was that the department was not able to honour the expectations of other agencies to whom clients owed accounts, and the rent arrears of many client families had grown despite the help and support of the children's department. The best example of difficulties here is illustrated by the changing relationship with the housing department:

The housing department notifies the children's department of any orders for possession which have been obtained, which gives the children's department three to four weeks in which to investigate and see if anything can be done to help the family to stave off eviction or find alternative accommodation. Occasionally families are referred by the housing department for assistance before the possession order stage is reached, because they are felt to have special problems. The children's department frequently collects rents from families and also receives and holds money for rent where the housing department cannot accept it because a notice to quit has been issued. [Reply to original questionnaire.]

Apparently, despite good co-operation

. . . the main grounds for contention have been that the housing department frequently cancels evictions at the request of the children's department and runs the risk of accumulating further arrears as a result of this. A rent guarantee scheme is in the process of evolution in order to meet this objection in certain cases.

Problems also arose through Part III emergency accommodation becoming inadequate and so causing children to be admitted to care because of homelessness. At the same time the problems defined in a joint circular from the Ministry of Health, the Home Office and the Ministry of Housing and Local Government of 31 October 1966 on *Temporary Accommodation for Homeless Families* drew attention to the need for improved facilities for those families. Locally, a report had been made to the prevention sub-committee meeting of the children's department in December 1966, raising the question of responsibility for social case work in respect of families in Part III accommodation. The welfare services committee was responsible for Part III accommodation, but in its minute expressed the view that responsibility for case work help for families with children should rest with the children's officer. There was also a minute from the housing department suggesting that, in cases involving children, the children's committee should indemnify the rent, and that, where possible, the family should be rehoused in sub-standard accommodation.

A joint report on the *Homeless Families* circular was then drawn up by the Medical Officer of Health, the director of welfare services, the housing manager and the children's officer in January 1967. It was observed that only recently, for the first time for many years, had children been admitted to care because of eviction. The number of families needing emergency accommodation had grown from eleven to twenty-five in Milltown between March 1962 and March 1966. Eviction orders were increasingly being notified to the children's department, and the report continued:

Another interesting fact which emerges is that, of the three families evicted, one was not visited, one was believed to have referred the problem to the officer of another agency (but had not in fact done so) and the third was the 'Smith' family, a report on whom is attached and whom it was quite impossible to help at that late stage. These admittedly limited numbers suggested two points; firstly that visiting families under threat of eviction is well worth doing. Many families, when contacted, appear only dimly aware of the reality of the threat or else are taking no steps to avert it. Timely help may enable them either to raise all or part of the money required, or to take steps to find other accommodation. The situation of these families is aggravated by the fact that once a notice to quit has been issued, and sometimes apparently even before, the housing department refuses to accept money from them and many of them are quite unable to hold on to the limited sums which they could raise. The children's department workers are able to collect any money as and when it is available and hold it for the families.

The report went on to draw attention to thirty-four further families, all at risk from a housing point of view, where the children's department already held the rent books. It was estimated that the total number of children at risk from homelessness was about two hundred. The situation was seen as mainly concerned with large lower-income families, some with very low ability to cope. Possible causes of the difficulties were described as follows:

1. High rents of new council accommodation.
2. Rents of older council property rising rapidly.
3. Cheaply rented privately owned accommodation being rapidly demolished.
4. The current economic situation resulting in increased unemployment with effects possibly most marked in the low income group.

The report went on to suggest changes in housing policy towards the provision of lower-rented housing, or the introduction of a rent rebate scheme, and more flexibility in the practice of paying off arrears. It also recommended that notice be given to the children's department of all eviction orders immediately they were obtained and, wherever possible, that families in arrears and likely to be in more than temporary difficulties should be referred at an earlier stage to the children's department. Case work services were considered necessary for families in Part III accommodation. Case work had been provided in the past by the children's department for families already known to them, and for other families with children, when requested by welfare services, or any other agency. However, it was felt that a full case work service to cover the needs of the homeless and potentially homeless should now include:

1. Early referral of families threatened with eviction.
2. Families where an immediate threat had been overcome but longer-term support was needed.
3. Evicted families in temporary accommodation.
4. Families who have been rehoused from temporary accommodation.

Suggested changes in temporary accommodation were that Part III accommodation be used for emergency cases only; that units housing up to six families each could be established on lines suggested in the joint Ministries' circular on *Homeless Families*; and that 'intermediate' houses in stages (possibly up to about twenty eventually) should be provided with more flexible renting, and these should not be confused with sub-standard housing. Such intermediate housing could be used imaginatively, and ghettos of problem families could be avoided.

An interesting case study of a family in Part III accommodation (the Smith family referred to) was quoted as an example of the difficulties which some families were experiencing, difficulties beyond their immediate capacity to control:

Report on the Smith family

Mr Smith, coal merchant's labourer.
Mrs Smith.
Eight children aged 4–19.

Tne Smiths approached the children's department and shortly afterwards were referred to the housing department under the usual procedure for notification of pending eviction. An eviction order was obtained against the family and expired. The arrears of rent to that date were £45.

On investigation it was found that Mr Smith's wages averaged £10 per week and the eldest son, aged 19 years, contributed £3 per week. The Family Allowance was £2 11s 0d. The family had no other resources and it appeared impossible for them to raise the necessary sum in the time available. The weekly rent was £2 3s 6d, which in itself was too much for this family's income. The housing department was unwilling to accept anything less than the full amount owing and in view of the large sum involved they could not accept the Smiths' offer to pay something off the arrears each week.

As Mr Smith had done two years' National Service, enquiries were made from the Soldiers', Sailors' and Airmen's Families Association regarding a possible grant. The secretary of the SSAFA did not think the chances of raising such a large amount were very good but an appointment was made for Mr Smith, which unfortunately he did not keep. It was felt, however, that the advisability of clearing the arrears from charitable sources was in any case questionable as it seemed unlikely that the family could afford to pay this rent in future.

The Smiths made some effort to find alternative accommodation but were not successful, and Mrs Smith and the six youngest children were admitted to Part III accommodation. (One son was in a detention centre.) Mr Smith went to relations and the eldest child obtained a flat.

There is now some possibility that the 19 year old will not return, even if the family is rehoused, thus reducing the family income even further. Mrs Smith is thinking of going out to work, but, in any case, it is not felt that either a wife's wages or a working child's wages, in these circumstances, can be relied upon in assessing a family's resources.

This means, in effect, that the family's only reliable income for two adults and seven dependent children is about £12 10s 0d per week. It seems clear that they are barely in a position to pay any rent at all if they are to be adequately fed and clothed, and at the present time it is difficult to see a solution to their problem. It is calculated that if Mr Smith had been in receipt of a National Assistance allowance at the full rate before the eviction he would have received £16 8s 0d exclusive of the Family Allowance of £2 11s 0d. His total income, based on the Assistance Board scale, would therefore have been £18 19s 6d, from which a few shillings would have been deducted for the working child.

The Smiths have other difficulties—there are some other debts, the housing department reports that home standards were poor and shortly after the family's reception into Part III accommodation a son was sent to a detention centre for three months as a result of breaking and entering offences.

It is noteworthy, however, that prior to this period of crisis the family seem never to have been drawn to the attention of any of the social services in the town. This would suggest that, despite any difficulties, they were a reasonably well functioning family and that the precipitating crisis was the result of an increasingly untenable economic position.

As a result of these discussions and considerations the town council on 1 February 1967 passed a resolution calling on their Members of Parliament to press for higher family allowances, as homelessness was felt to be caused largely by inadequate family income.

Eventually it was resolved that a rent indemnity scheme should be operated and brought into existence from 1 April 1967. This scheme gave powers to the children's department to indemnify the housing department for twelve months in specially selected cases, for example:

1. Where a family due for eviction is rehoused in lower-rented accommodation.
2. Where, because of the children, the family is allowed to continue to occupy the house, although in debt with arrears of rent.
3. Where a family with children is evicted from a house not owned by the corporation and rehoused to prevent admission of children into care.

To give the arrangement status it was decided that the client would be asked to sign a declaration accepting twelve months' supervision from the children's department, whose worker would collect the rent. The council decided that clients should not be aware that if

C

they failed to pay rent during this period the children's department would pay it for them.

It will be seen that the rent guarantee scheme came about in Milltown through pressure from the housing department to be indemnified against loss. The children's department could both provide the indemnity and at the same time further the development of its preventive work. The children's department was also now entitled to ask the housing department for up to twenty 'intermediate houses' for use where it was felt that families were living in accommodation which was too expensive for them. The financial estimate for rent guarantees was fixed at £300 a year for an experimental period, and the family care officer had the power to decide who would receive a rent guarantee. However, although the department held seventy-two rent books in February 1969, most of these rents were collected without the use of the guarantee scheme. In Milltown, at the time of our research, of the eight families who were helped under the rent guarantee scheme, only one had failed to respond, and this family, on being served with a notice for eviction, was eventually able to find the necessary money. The twenty 'intermediate' houses were actually never required by the children's department to help with their work.

The fact that policy with regard to financial grants—loans or rent indemnities—was based on the experience of the specialised family care section has had some repercussions on the policy affecting what aid is available for the work of the officers concerned with children after they come into care (work referred to as 'rehabilitation') and there is a similar reluctance to spend money. Grants are not easily available for rehabilitating or restorative work —that is, for work to help families in need who have children in care, so that the children may return home. Other forms of material aid are used instead. Second-hand furniture or blankets are given freely by individual officers after consultation with a senior officer. The department has a good deal of second-hand clothing, too, which is given out individually and through jumble sales held for families at the department's group work centre. On the whole, money is spent only to prevent homelessness, and material goods are given to prevent a breakdown in family care or to enable a child to go back home.

In Milltown the stringency of financial policy makes written guide lines irrelevant. The committee is strict with estimates, but the policy about the amount of financial aid to be given in the form of loans is based primarily on the experience of staff. This was stated in the reply to the original questionnaire as follows:

Prior to the 1963 Act the department had been obliged to solve problems without recourse to direct financial aid, and its preventive service had been established on a family case work basis. It is hoped that it is not innate conservatism alone which has led to the continuation of this policy with little substantial alteration. Some initial difficulty was experienced after the passing of the Act, owing to the increased expectations of both clients and other departments and agencies (more especially the latter), but this has been to a large extent resolved. It is still difficult at times to convince other bodies that the amount of aid given is a matter for decision by the local children committee and has to be included in estimates, and that there is not an unlimited reservoir of money available which can be drawn upon at will.

It also seems that insufficient emphasis has been placed on the phrase 'in exceptional circumstances' in the Act and that a widespread impression has been created that it is the duty of the children's department to provide almost unlimited assistance in a wide variety of circumstances.

The policy of stringency which limits expenditure was seen as giving a firm framework to the workers and relieving them of the considerable anxiety which can be experienced about whether to give or withold assistance, particularly in view of the continual 'demand' they experienced for help with gas and electricity bills. If grants cannot be given, and loans are limited in amount, the area of financial intervention is strictly limited. The general feeling was that the arbitrary power to give or withhold money is inappropriate to the exercise of child care case work, with its relationship of trust and support giving confidence, understanding and hope to a client to enable him to cope with the task of bringing up the children.

Staff developed their own guide lines about recommending a case for a rent guarantee or for a loan. They considered that a good rent guarantee case was a large family, with no alternative accommodation, where there was a possibility of collecting the money back because the client was responsive to casework help. The fact that the committee had delegated the powers to give loans, because the amounts were so small, meant also that individual workers could, on their own assessment, help families whose problems were not regarded sympathetically by the community at large. When asked what sort of cases were unsuitable for help, workers thought these were large 'unco-operative' families who never made a consistent effort to pay their debts, or the family whose income was so low that regular payment of rent would be unrealistic; families with a reasonable income where help could be obtained by other means, for example, by requesting creditors to stay their hand; families who had no reasonable prospect of paying regularly; families who would use the rent scheme as a substitute for more effective case work help. However, case work and the rent indemnity scheme were not always considered entirely incompatible. Staff thought that the signing of the declaration and the commitment implied could help to build up client responsibility, and involved the client closely in the plan of working together towards some goal in which he shared. The guarantee scheme was thought to have some advantages in the case work plan. First, it was of crucial importance in keeping the family's home together, and second, regular visiting to collect the rent meant that a relationship could be built up between client and worker which could be used to help the client generally to cope better with his day-to-day problems. However, other workers did say that a major disadvantage of the scheme was the focus on rent, and paying rent, which changed the nature of the relationship; the relationship of trust could break down if the rent guarantee was withdrawn, and it was then impossible to continue effective casework.

Similarly, staff developed their own guide lines about the giving of loans. In practice loans were given to all kinds of families in emergencies and crisis situations, mainly where the families needed food or fuel or the mother was distracted by her problems. On the whole, they were given to clients well known to the department, and a second loan was not given until the first was repaid.

Preventive goals are implicit; after that the principle behind the giving of all financial aid was that the clients were unable to get help elsewhere. However, the department's housing indemnity scheme has led to problems arising with the Gas and Electricity Boards in Milltown when families have incurred debts to them. The Electricity Board, for example, cuts off the electricity supply for non-payment of bills and will not reconnect it until payment has been made. The children's department, however, does not use its powers to pay the arrears of debt, and has no arrangement to indemnify these national boards comparable to that devised for indemnifying the local housing committee. The county surrounding Milltown is occasionally prepared to pay such arrears when appropriate, and this has led to difficulties in relationships and co-operation with the boards which had not previously been experienced.

On the other hand, as was pointed out by staff, the department does seem able to achieve its ends by slow case work methods without resorting to large grants or loans.

All the family case workers had contact with the Electricity Board, the Gas Board, the housing department and to some extent other creditors. The part this contact played in their work ranged from a very large part to a very small part. The main object was the endeavour to keep the family situation financially sound by negotiating with a creditor, and an attempt would be made to sort out the problem. There was general satisfaction about the relationship with the housing department, but workers wished it was practicable or possible for there to be greater co-operation with Gas and Electricity Boards. However, it was recognised that these were commercial undertakings with no welfare functions, whose bills could not be written off. One specific complaint was the fact that the Electricity Board would not put in a pre-payment meter until the last quarterly bill had been paid.

The majority of staff had regular contact with the SB officers. This contact played quite a big part in their work, especially while a worker was on office duty, when apparently a number of inarticulate clients bring queries to the department and the worker needs to contact the SB officers to help clarify the situation. The SB officers are also approached to see if they are in a position to give grants to various families, and they are sometimes contacted for an exchange of information. Over the last few years the quality of this contact has changed and there is better understanding and mutual trust. Apparently the Social Security office is now seen as more willing to pay gas, electricity and rent arrears in certain cases, and the new manager is seen as being much more sympathetic. This change was welcomed, the general opinion being that workers would like to see a continuation of the growing flexibility, co-ordination and co-operation from the Social Security office, with more personal contacts and possibily with the SB officers resuming attendance at case conferences.

On more specific issues, it was felt that it would be helpful if the SB officers would more often discuss with child care workers any exceptional method of paying allowances; for example, whether they intended to pay the rent direct to the house owner or the tenant, whether it would be desirable to pay the money to the mother, and so on. One worker felt very strongly that it was unrealistic for the SB officers to call the man the head of the household, and that many situations would be improved by paying full allowances to the woman. Workers were concerned about clients who came to the department after having been refused a payment by the Social Security office, and when the children's department telephoned it was found that some payment could, in fact, be made. It was also suggested that SB officers still differentiated between the 'deserving' and the 'undeserving'.

All workers had some contact with voluntary relief-giving agencies, but contact here was not as frequent as with the Social Security office. Often workers would approach voluntary societies if the SB officers could not give a family a grant. There were mixed feelings as to whether the practice of channelling all requests for aid through the Milltown Council of Social Service was really satisfactory. In some instances it was thought it would be more appropriate to approach the lord mayors' funds and Forces' benevolent funds direct. We had the impression that letters for help from the WRVS were given fairly freely by workers, after only a perfunctory enquiry, if a client asked for one and if he was on supplementary benefits. One worker clearly had the impression that the SB officers sent people to the children's department for second-hand clothing or a WRVS note before they gave a discretionary grant.

Since 1963 there had been very little in the way of changes of practice in working with the voluntary societies, but the following problems were raised. Some funds had outlived their original purposes and could not be drawn on easily. There was need for an extension of means to provide holidays for poor families and it was also suggested that a family welfare association which gave aid and case work would benefit the town.

Perhaps the most striking consistency about the workers' views was their general belief that case work and relief-giving were incompatible and distorted the function of the children's department. The department did not publicise the small amount of financial aid it gave, or its general powers to give financial aid, and workers were particularly uncommunicative about the rent guarantee scheme.

Clients were asked not to tell the rest of the estate if they were benefiting from it. The workers were concerned that if their powers were widely known the demands made would be very heavy, and the service would be unable to meet them and unable to give time to anything else but the consideration of these demands.

We then looked in detail at the sort of families helped under the new powers. A sample of cases was examined and analysed into the following groups:

Group 1. Preventive cases that had received financial aid.

Group 2. Preventive cases that had received material aid or assistance in kind.

Group 3. Preventive cases that had not received any aid.

In Milltown the major form which financial aid took was expenditure for food (67 per cent of cases). The next most common form was a rent guarantee (28 per cent), and a small number were helped by expenditure on fuel (6 per cent). Most financial aid was given as a loan (72 per cent), and often help of this kind was given more than once (67 per cent). The families were very poor. The amounts of known income of the families, most of which (83 per cent) consisted of four or five children living at home, was under £20 a week, and the majority (71 per cent) were in fact living on or below a subsistence standard of living. Just over a quarter (28 per cent) were dependent on the father's earnings, and nearly a quarter (22 per cent) were receiving a supplementary benefits allowance subject to a wage stop (that is, the allowance was held down so that the man would not receive more in benefit that he had received while working). The rest were dependent upon supplementary or insurance benefit. Generally (77 per cent) the father was an unskilled manual worker. There were few (6 per cent) cohabitations, half the unions were legal marriages (55 per cent), and the rest were fathers (11 per cent) or mothers (28 per cent) coping alone. The great majority (94 per cent) lived in local authority rented accommodation.

Over a third of the families were currently receiving help from other agencies, mainly from health visitors, education departments and probation officers. Fewer than half the families (44 per cent) had free school meals for all the children. Nearly a quarter had a child who had appeared before the juvenile court during the previous five years and 80 per cent had had a child in care. Interestingly enough, although the families helped financially were so poor and were known to so many agencies, half of them came of their own accord to the children's department and were not referred by any other agencies. The financial help given was mostly (72 per cent) below £5, and conditions were attached to it in almost all cases (94 per cent).

The reasons or grounds on which the department decided to give financial aid on a preventive basis were largely the maintenance of material standards (61 per cent), to ease the housing problem (41 per cent) and to be supportive of the families' efforts (11 per cent). Maintenance of material standards here meant generally money for food to help the family until the next supplementary benefit or Family Allowance payment. The goals towards which worker and client worked with the use of financial aid were in the short term (50 per cent) towards a solution of the housing problem, and in the long term (72 per cent) to enable the parents to cope properly with their parental task. Examples were given as follows of some workers' goals in particular cases:

Short-term goal

Getting family rehoused. Getting myself accepted by very unstable, aggressive father. Encouraging two oldest children to attend school more regularly.

When re-opened after closure of few months, to help mother over depressive stage and help both husband and wife to cope with pending court case (fraudulently obtaining Ministry of Social Security supplementary benefits) by giving help of supportive nature.

Long-term goal

To improve mother's attitude towards children. She had been repeatedly asking for them to be taken into care, and was especially rejecting towards the older child. Case work aim was to help her to apply the considerable insight she already possessed.

To help family over financial matters, especially over the rent, and to help them to take responsibility of seeing rent, etc, paid regularly, by case worker collecting debts. Also to lend support to a very young and inexperienced mother during father's frequent absences from home. To try and get father to face up to responsibility towards family.

Intensive support on long-term basis to help low mentality parents cope with large family.

The workers considered that they were invariably (100 per cent) successful in attaining their first goal and moderately successful (39 per cent) in attaining their long-term goal, though in a good many cases there had not been sufficient time to make an assessment yet. However, success was thought to be due not to the financial aid of the department alone, but rather to the supportive help of the worker, who intervened with debt-collecting bodies such as the Gas and Electricity Boards, collected the debts on the boards' behalf from the client, and in doing so helped specifically with some change in the family attitude or ability to cope.

In the second group of families, where the help given was not financial but consisted of goods in some form, such as clothing or furniture, the families were not in quite such a desperate financial situation, though still very poor. Nearly half (45 per cent were on or below subsistence level, a significant number (13 per cent) were on the wage stop exercised by the SBC. On balance, the families tended to have four or more children at home under 18, with a fairly high proportion of children (47 per cent) who had previously been in care. Nearly half the families (47 per cent) were a married union dependent on the father's income (40 per cent), and just over half (52 per cent) the fathers were unskilled manual workers. The general picture was one of families well known to the children's department, and material aid had been given to them before (54 per cent). In this group 40 per cent of the families lived in accommodation rented from private landlords, and it may be that this factor influenced the giving of second-hand goods rather than including the group in the rent guarantee scheme or even giving a small financial loan. This group of families was referred in a different way from the first group. Only a small number (20 per cent) came on their own; some were referred by members of the public who must have known something of the department's practice; the majority were referred from other social services.

The main short-term goals were helping parents to cope (33 per cent) and easing the housing problem (33 per cent). In the long term the main goal was again helping parents to cope or fulfil their responsibility (93 per cent). Workers felt they had been successful in the short term (87 per cent) but in the long term in the majority of cases (53 per cent) there was not sufficient time to tell. However, a significant proportion (27 per cent) were unsuccessful in the long term in this group. This compares very significantly with the first group, where there was no more success in the long term, and highlights the complexity of the problems of the families who received material but no financial aid.

In comparison, the group of families with whom the case workers tried to prevent break-up and which received no aid at all is interesting. There was no family known definitely to be on the wage stop and only 13 per cent were receiving supplementary benefits. 22 per cent were below the short-term subsistence rate, however. The largest number (46 per cent) were dependent on the father's earnings. Here was the lowest percentage of married families (40 per cent); a number (40 per cent) were one-parent families, and the majority (73 per cent) had three or fewer children. Only a small number (20 per cent) had children away from home, and these were mainly from the one-parent families. Such children were in care mainly for parental desertion or short-term illness. This group contained the only immigrant families in the sample (two Anglo-West Indians). A third of the families (33 per cent) were classed as unskilled manual workers and a third were semi-skilled. While still largely living in council rented housing (73 per cent), this group contained the only example of owner-occupied housing. In this group the case workers' main short-term goals, in working preventively without aid, were to ease the housing problem (53 per cent), and their long-term goals were to help families cope better as parents (67 per cent). They considered that in the short term they were entirely successful (100 per cent), but were less hopeful about the future (39 per cent). Thus the main long-term goal in all the groups was to improve the parents' ability to cope or fulfil their responsibilities.

So the total picture which emerges is clearly one of help being given where the need is greatest, and help being differentiated according to diagnosis. Financial aid went to the poorest families, in the most stable unions, with four to five children under 9 years at home, and where the families were tenants of corporation houses who would have to be evicted if the rent were not paid. Material goods were given to a group of families who were also very poor but in less poverty than the first group (though with a similar number of children), a good proportion of whom were renting accommodation from private landlords. The group which received no aid at all were mainly in council house accommodation but were in less financial distress and had fewer children at home.

Our survey showed that in a sample of families' incomes taken on 14 June 1968 61 per cent of those given loans or rent guarantees were on or below the poverty line (equivalent of 'scale rate plus rent' paid by the SBC). Poverty is a constant factor in the preventive work; the relief given by the department is small. It seems to have been the possibility of widespread demand arising out of poverty in the families, and the small budget of the children's department, which circumscribed Milltown's interpretation of the Act and influenced its case work practice and perhaps also its beliefs about the incompatibility of financial aid and case work. The town's case workers saw their preventive case work task as enabling families to cope better with the task of bringing up their children, understanding children's development and difficulties, and fostering better relationships within the family unit. The first essential was seen as providing for the security of a house in which to live, the provision of shelter being basic to family life and historically the province and protective function of the children's department. But in seeking to promote the basic security for the family the direction of their work was largely defined by the policy of the housing committee and the inadequacy and unsatisfactory nature of Part III accommodation. Subsidiary to this, prevention involved case work to better the relationships and coping capacities within the family, and other agencies were regarded as more appropriate for the disbursement of financial aid or providing financial independence. There was, however, clearly anxiety, ambivalence and uncertainty in the attitude of the workers to giving money, which may have been an important influence in the formation of departmental policy.

The most important effect of the 1963 Act on the practice of Milltown Workers has been the introduction of the power to guarantee rents where necessary for a small number of families whose home life would otherwise be broken by eviction, and the extension of this practice to the giving of loans which would help maintain the family through an emergency. This kind of help, and the provision of clothing, bedding, furniture, etc, was given to families who were estimated to be able to use the help and who would gain a feeling of support, hope and confidence from the receipt of it, so increasing their own ability to cope better and fulfil their parental responsibilities. When giving financial aid, the officers responded to families in the greatest financial need[1] where lack of

[1] See the analysis of sample cases in Appendix 3 for evidence of this.

food and lack of housing are clearly linked with the prevention of child neglect and admission to care. This situation was realistic for the workers but raised the broader question of how effective their help and work could be in the presence of continuing poverty among the families.

5. Nordale

Before 1963 Nordale had also begun to work on preventive lines, mainly because of the shortage of accommodation in local authority children's homes, and its conviction that substitute family care was 'second best' care. But another operative factor in prevention was the number of children received into care between 1950 and 1960 because their parents had been evicted and not considered eligible for Part III accommodation—accommodation provided for families rendered homeless in circumstances which could not reasonably have been foreseen. And so in 1960 the housing committee agreed to sub-let three houses to the children's committee, provided that committee were responsible for the rents. Thus Nordale was the first authority in the North-west region to experiment with housing management linked to prevention and rehabilitation, since these houses were used to re-unite children in care with their parents.

The 1963 Act coincided with the negotiations with the National Family Service Unit to establish a unit in the town. Because of the shortage of FSU workers at that time, however, these plans proved abortive and the council agreed that a family case work unit should be established within the children's department, but operating as a distinct team, with family case workers carrying small case loads not exceeding fifteen. The workers were to carry out the preventive work of the department with the hard core of multi-problem families as well as the rehabilitative work aimed at restoring the child to his family.

Financial aid was given cautiously at first because of the general anxiety that the demand would overwhelm the department. The original estimate was for £200 a year, which was to rise through succeeding years to £500. Amounts above £5, and then £10, were subject to the approval of both the chairman and vice-chairman of the committee. The children's officer or her deputy was authorised to spend within these limits, and the organiser of the family case work unit had similar powers.

In the beginning policy was in favour of giving loans rather than grants, but each case was examined by the workers in the light of specific needs.

Policy is strongly orientated to making loans. However, it is recognised that a proportion of expenditure is irrecoverable, whether advanced for rent guarantee or to relieve other needs, and consideration is given to each individual case in the light of individual circumstances. Grants of small amounts are disbursed for crisis requirements or to enable children from socially deprived and poor families to participate in community/youth/leisure activities. Grants are also made to enable friends or relatives to care temporarily for children . . .

We have noted significant differences in the attitude of clients receiving case work help and those helped in emergency situations. The former have a better record of repayment than the latter. This has helped to clarify policy. So far there has been no sustained pressure on clients to recover loans but we are currently considering action in possibly one or two cases (a fractional minority).   [Answers to questionnaire.]

Grants and loans were made for such varied items as household necessities, reconditioned washing machines, cookers, food, the transport of second-hand furniture, children's holidays, rent arrears, fines, electricity bills, fuel, decorating, etc. However, repayment difficulties led over the years towards a modification in policy resulting in fewer loans and more small grants, mainly for food in emergencies.

Material aid in kind was given freely to all kinds of families by the social workers, who were able to give second-hand clothing and furniture or food parcels without consultation at a higher level. Usually such goods were given to clients known to the department, and occasionally clients were asked to pay a nominal sum for this kind of aid. On the whole, workers had no objection to using this form of aid, provided the goods were in reasonable condition and the client wished to have them. It was pointed out that giving something to clients demonstrated that the department cared. However, clients' reactions to material aid were reported as mixed. Clothing of a good standard, particularly for children, was very welcome. But one worker felt that clients should be enabled to show any negative feelings about the situation. It was recognised that clients could see second-hand goods as a reflection of how other people judged their worth. Sometimes jumble sales were organised and items sold at 3d each; in this case clients had a choice and the appearance of charity was avoided.

As we have seen, Nordale already had in existence a rent guarantee scheme restricted initially to families occupying the three houses sub-let to the children committee and used for purposes of family rehabilitation. The success of this pilot scheme resulted in the council approving the purchase of additional scattered properties under Part V of the Housing Act, 1957, which were handed over to the children committee for them to manage and let, conditional on the children committee bearing the full cost of property maintenance and any arrears of rent which might accrue.

In 1967 Nordale council decided that it was more appropriate to use powers under Section 1 of the Children and Young Persons Act, 1963, to purchase houses rather than under Part V of the Housing Act, 1957. Between 1967 and 1969 some thirty houses in all were managed and let by the children committee. The majority had been specially purchased but a few were acquired by the estates committee in advance of slum clearance and sub-let on a temporary basis to the children committee. The power of management carried with it the obligation that any shortfall of rent or other financial liability was a charge on the children committee. This was in effect a rent guarantee and a tenancy guarantee seen from the client's viewpoint. The arguments supporting this policy were that the cost of caring for families at risk should be shared by the community at large and not by a section of people in council houses. Also, the existence of a different pool of houses allowed greater flexibility as regards letting which was of special use in accommodating families evicted from the private sector who were not registered with the council, and those families who occasionally appeared without warning from other parts of the country.

An integral part of the agreement between the two Nordale committees was that families could be moved into council houses when there was evidence that they were caring satisfactorily for their children and paying the rent. This policy was not free of difficulties, and the following report spelt out in detail the issues raised by the Milltown workers:

In accordance with committee policy it is conditional that any family given the tenancy of a Children Authority house should be prepared to accept case work help. This is fully discussed before the family moves in and no one has ever refused to co-operate, but this should not blind us to the fact that threatened or actual homelessness constitutes undue pressure on the client to consent to case work, and subsequently even though the client has agreed initially the contract is not necessarily successful, nor is it binding.

The conflict for the case worker is equally open-minded and can prove painful because of the importance attached by members of council to helping or conditioning a client to pay the rent regularly. The traditional role of case worker is to accept the client without criticism or judgment, to make a trusting relationship and to allow the client self-determination. This concept does not equate with the role of agent of the landlord who can and will evict if rent arrears reach too high a ceiling, or if minimum standards of social acceptance are not attained.

It is easy for most social workers to identify with the 'under-dog' tenant against the 'bad' landlord, and indeed this has been the traditional role in the past, when much social work was pioneered in high-density areas of decaying housing, squalor and exploitation. It is not easy for the social worker when his or her own agency is seen to be the landlord, particularly when houses in poor structural conditions are being managed and let. In such circumstances the children's department is seen as landlord and the case worker, as mediator, can readily become the scapegoat for client–tenant resentment, and lead to deliberate withholding of rent, deliberate non-co-operation about attending clinics or sending children to school.

Case work techniques encourage in some cases controlled 'acting out' against authority and working through immature patterns of rebellion, but it is very difficult when the authority figure is the children's officer or the children's committee.

Conflicting loyalties between agency and client could tear the case worker apart in any agency where the professional social worker's judgment is not respected or considered. When confronted by non-payment of rent, taking in lodgers without consent, destroying or damaging property and other anti-social acts, the case worker has to assess the level of maturity the client has reached, and how much pressure a tired mother or mentally ill father can stand. If, for example, the regular payment of rent is seen as the paramont and primary objective, the concept of on-going diagnosis and treatment is frustrated from the outset.

Although these difficulties were acknowledged, there was agreement that the opportunity to manage this pool of houses made a very positive contribution in the drive to keep families together.

In 1966 the housing and children's committees also reached agreement about the importance of taking steps to prevent eviction from council houses and decided that families with serious rent arrears in council properties 'were to be notified to the children's department, in order that inquiries could be made and advice and help offered. If it was considered to be in the interest of the family, the rent could be guaranteed by the children's committee. As a matter of policy it was implicit that no rent should be guaranteed without case work help and supervision.' However, the large number of cases referred to the children's department meant that the implementation of guaranteed rents for council houses laid such a burden of additional social enquiry and rent collection on the staff that it became impossible to deal properly with the referrals 'at the case work depth demanded'. There was a differential diagnosis to be made about each case of rent arrears in council houses, the workers found. Many families did not need casework help but rather more assiduous and determined rent collection; the problems were primarily problems of housing management. Further discussions took place and resulted in an increase of staff in both the housing and children's departments so that referral to case workers of serious rent arrear cases were seen to be selective. In a number of chronic cases rent guarantees were given to allow time for case workers to be accepted by the families and to identify the problems.

However, by 1969 the opinion of the department was that rent guarantees operating for normal council tenants were appropriate for only two categories of problem: first, in exceptional cases where one or both parents suffer from severe mental or physical handicaps; second, when the authority has no other means of preventing otherwise well adjusted children from coming into care. It was felt that rent guarantees 'lull the family into a false sense of security and prolong the client's phantasy that eviction will not take place'. Far better success was experienced by intensive case work with families in serious rent arrears without the rents being guaranteed, and after careful consideration it was decided to terminate existing rent guarantees for council houses, giving adequate warning to clients. The department preferred the policy of controlling a number of houses and collecting rents rather than offering rent guarantees, and found this a more effective means of help.

It will be seen that Nordale's policy was evolved from the experience of the practice of case workers and the assessments they made. There were no written directions within the department, which was not a large one, but policy was kept consistent by staff meetings with the children's officer and close supervision of the work by the officers in charge. The existence of a small, specialised

D

family case work unit facilitated the gathering of facts and information and skilled examination of what was involved in practice.[1]

Everyone accepted the view that financial aid should be given
only as part of a case work plan. Money was rarely given, and then
generally only in a crisis—for example, to provide food for a
family deserted by the father and left without money during the
weekend. Except where families were already known to the
department, it was felt that clients should not know that the
department had the power to give financial aid, as they might get a
false impression of its resources and put new members of staff
into a difficult position by refusing. In answer to an original
questionnaire the merits and demerits of loans, grants and guarantees were outlined as follows:

We attempt to evaluate our policy from time to time and the consensus
of opinion is that there has not been much abuse of Section 1 and that
the administrative policy at present is flexible enough to be effective
and enabling. My staff and I see inherent dangers in the promiscuous
exercise of power under this section as follows:

(*a*) Public opinion might be roused and become hostile.
(*b*) The Children's Authority could usurp the function of the
       Ministry of Social Security.
(*c*) We could be acting *ultra vires* in the sense of acting outside the
       law in certain categories of referral (e.g. to pay court fines to
       prevent a parent going to prison, to pay electricity or gas charges
       where there have been breaking offences).
(*d*) We feel strongly that any financial help should preferably be
       allied to case work, although we have given material help, par-
       ticularly items of furniture, prams, etc, more freely and excep-
       tionally small sums of money or goods to help 'floating' clients
       in crisis situations.
(*e*) We are aware of social needs which demand action by the
       government and subscribe to a broad policy of applying pressure
       on the Ministry of Social Security (*vis à vis* Child Poverty Action
       Group) and seeking to influence local government policy (e.g.
       to inaugurate a rent rebate scheme) rather than giving *ad hoc*
       help to individuals who are fortunate enough to know of and
       qualify for help by the children's department under Section 1.
(*f*) Too permissive a policy might open the doors to a flood tide
       of applicants.

Of the families who received financial aid in the course of preventive work, 70 per cent of the sample in Nordale were on or

[1] See Sylvia Cox, 'Housing schemes in children's departments', *Case
Conference*, vol. 16, No. 11.

below the poverty line, and it would seem, therefore, that the grants
and loans and rent guarantees were part of a case work plan which
included the temporary alleviation of poverty, while recognising
that national measures were needed for its permanent relief. The
ideal type of case for preventive financial aid was not assessed by
poverty alone but also by considering whether the family was
likely to surmount its difficulties with financial help, and was really
trying to help itself. Other important criteria were distress and
poverty caused by unforeseen circumstances, or long-term economy
which would operate by saving the cost of children in care or
rehousing. Inappropriate situations for financial aid were thought
to fall into three categories: those where the father's irresponsible
spending of money was the main problem, those where the client
tried to manipulate the case worker, and those where clients had
not benefited from previous financial aid. The department's practice
led the children's officer to make recommendations to her committee which could in turn affect the policy of other council
committees.

Family advice functions within the children's department

Month by month the attention of the children's committee is drawn
to the high incidence of problems associated with housing in general
and dealt with by child care officers. The figures show that there is no
room for complacency or belief that needs are being fully met in the
town. It seems to us that there are not enough houses at a rent which
is fair for families who have a low earning capacity and a large number
of children, and that there may well be a strong case for the council
to consider adopting a rent rebate scheme with a view to encouraging
some existing tenants to move out and make way for those whose needs
are particularly pressing and who for one reason and another are not
in a position to secure accommodation by their own efforts.

Recommendations

1. Efforts should be intensified to find a suitable property for con-
   version into two self-contained furnished flats for instant but
   short-term occupation.
2. There should be further consideration of the needs of clients
   who have settled well in temporary accommodation and how
   this would affect overall policy.
3. Representations should be made through appropriate channels
   that rent or rent arrears should in hard-core cases be deducted
   at source (by the SBC) or by attachment of wages.
4. Marginally it may be necessary to accept that one or two families
   with unusual degrees of handicap or pathology should be sup-

ported by the community rent-free in the same way as the Ministry of Labour decides that some inadequate fathers cannot be expected to work.

It is uneconomic use of a case worker's time to be visiting daily to collect rent and at the same time creating an image which pre-empts case work.

As we have seen, material aid in the form of second-hand cloth-ing and furniture was given freely without the need for consultation at a higher level, and usually given to clients known to the department. In making decisions about giving goods the practice of the family case work unit was influential. The senior worker organised weekly discussions on families with problems, where the question of giving financial or material aid would be raised. All the workers were satisfied with the guidance they had about the policy for giving such help and felt that the limits of the depart-ment's resources, the personal guidance of senior officers and the general objectives of their work left them in no doubt about the appropriateness of such help when it was given. The fact that money was limited made them selective, and they knew that money must be given only in the context of preventing admission to care or family break-up, particularly where a large family was involved.

In Nordale most financial aid shown by the sample of cases was given for food (40 per cent of cases), then for coal (20 per cent), bedding (10 per cent), household repairs (20 per cent) and rent support (10 per cent), and was given chiefly in the form of a loan (70 per cent). Only 10 per cent of cases involved rent guarantees. Conditions were attached to the loan in 40 per cent of the cases (the most frequent condition was to require repayment). The families were mainly (50 per cent) unskilled manual workers, the majority (70 per cent) living on or below the subsistence rate, and in 80 per cent of cases children were receiving free school meals. Just under a quarter (22 per cent) were on the wage stop. The main source of income was supplementary benefits (50 per cent), with 20 per cent dependent on the father's earnings. Again, the majority (90 per cent) were living in accommodation rented from the local authority, having lived in the area over five years (90 per cent). Half the families (50 per cent) were married unions with three of four children at home (50 per cent), though the extremes here ranged from eleven to two children. A very small number of the families in this group had referred themselves to the children's department. The main sources of referral were the NSPCC (40 per cent) and housing department (30 per cent). The majority (80 per cent) had never had any case work help from any other agencies; the rest had been helped by the NSPCC or the probation department. About a fifth of the families had a child who had appeared before the juvenile court during the previous five years, and the large majority (80 per cent) had had children in care or approved school during the last five years.

The main reasons given for which the department decided to give financial aid were: to maintain material standards (60 per cent), to ease the financial problem caused by low income (40 per cent), to be supportive to the family (30 per cent) and, to a lesser degree (20 per cent), to ease the housing problem and help with the difficulties of bringing up the children. The short-term goals were largely to improve the family's ability to cope and help the parents to fulfil their responsibilities (70 per cent) and to ease the housing problem (70 per cent); the long-term goal was also to increase the family's ability to cope and to improve the relationship within it (80 per cent). The workers thought they had been largely successful in attaining their short-term goals (80 per cent). In the long term 40 per cent of the cases were successful and in 40 per cent there was insufficient time to tell. The remainder (20 per cent) were unsuccessful.

In the second group, where families received material aid, mainly clothing or furniture, as part of the preventive case work, slightly under half the families (47 per cent) had parents who were married, and here were found most of the unsupported mothers (41 per cent). Three-quarters of these families had four or more children, a majority (65 per cent) had had children in care or an approved school during the last five years, and a good percentage (41 per cent) had children who had appeared in the juvenile court. The majority of families, where the income was known, were, however, on or below the subsistence rate (84 per cent) (see Appendix 3), though less (41 per cent) were in the class of unskilled manual workers and more (18 per cent) in the skilled category. Almost all the families (94 per cent), with the exception of a few (6 per cent) owner-occupiers, lived in local authority rented accommodation. Again the NSPCC seemed to have been particularly active in this town, referring 47 per cent of the families; afterwards housing, welfare and police were the principal referees.

The main short- and long-term goals were both to improve parental functioning. In the short-term most cases were thought to be successful (94 per cent); in the long term there had generally been insufficient time to tell (71 per cent). In this group, by comparison with the first, in significantly fewer cases (12 per cent) was there any positive success.

In the group of families who received no help at all the poverty was evidently not quite so striking; where the income was known, only 33 per cent were living at subsistence level. No families were known to be on the wage stop. The majority of the families (63 per cent) relied on the father's income, a good proportion of the fathers being skilled manual labourers (19 per cent). The most common number of children at home was three or four, and this group had the largest number (19 per cent) of older children (aged 10–18). The large majority (88 per cent) of these families had never had children in care. Half the families lived in accommodation rented from the local authority, a quarter (26 per cent) were owner-occupiers, and the rest were in privately rented accommodation. In this group the case workers' short-term and long-term goals were mainly the same—to improve the parents' ability to cope (37 per cent), to improve family relationships (31 per cent)—but there was an additional short-term goal: easing housing problems (25 per cent). In the short term the workers thought they had been successful in the majority of cases (88 per cent) but had not had sufficient time to judge whether the long-term goal had been achieved (75 per cent). The main reason for success was felt to be the support the case worker gave in helping the client towards some course of action which he could not pursue alone (56 per cent). Other important reasons for success were the fact that the department intervened with debt-collecting bodies (19 per cent), and that the case worker collected debts owing to other agencies. Important, too, was the case worker's focus on some aspect of change or modification in the family's attitude or ability to cope (31 per cent).

The study at Nordale is important in highlighting two factors. First, the powers provided by the Children and Young Persons Act, 1963, were used to give the department some management control over its clients' housing problems. And the method the department chose, in contrast to Milltown, was to acquire and control a number of houses which it could then let itself and collect the rents itself, rather than offer rent guarantees. Second, in this way the emphasis was firmly on the growth and self-reliance of the client as a tenant, with the enabling help of the specialised case worker. The department found from experience that clients responded to the resourcefulness, support and hope inherent in the case work relationship so that they were able to face the reality of what being a tenant means and to cope with it, even where there was extreme poverty and the disincentives were very great. The department was able to differentiate the clients who were not able to use case work help to cope with being tenants, and found the factors operating in non-payment of rent to be far more complex than poverty alone. In a report to the committee it drew attention to the problem in the following way:

Sixteen families needed every kind of assistance and sanction to induce rent payment. In thirteen of these families the income was uncertain, owing to the father working irregularly. In two cases there was no father and on one case father and mother were alcoholics and mentally unstable.

In all of the sixteen families there was evidence of misappropriation of income on excessive drinking and gambling, but, looking deeper, it was obvious that this hard core comprised people far more emotionally disturbed than the control group, with no 'frustration tolerance' to cope with adversity at work, minor illness, marital friction or poverty. For some reason their personality development had been arrested at the immature stage where immediate gratification needs must be met. Each of the clients could be diagnosed as having a character disorder. Six of thirty parents had had treatment for mental illness; nine of the fourteen fathers had been to prison for larceny, violence or incest.

A study of the thirty families who did pay their rent threw more light on the problem of rent failure. Sixteen of them had unsupported mothers and fifteen had no problem of misappropriation of income. The sixteenth was a prostitute who paid her rent from her earnings. Of the remaining twelve families, two fathers worked regularly. The incidence of mental illness and imprisonment was about the same; seven out of twelve fathers and one mother had been in prison, and ten out of forty parents had had psychiatric treatment in hospital.

It seems that separated or unsupported mothers manage, on the whole, very well as regards paying rent when they can rely on a steady income from the Ministry of Social Security, however low. Non-payment of rent in disturbed families is more a result of immaturity, early deprivation and in-built attitudes to rent-paying than low income, imprisonment or mental ill health.

The picture in Nordale is similar to that in Milltown, a picture of very poor families receiving financial and material aid, with financial aid going to those who most needed help and could best use it and where some crisis of management or circumstances had produced a real risk of child neglect, taking into account also the past history of the family. Nordale, from the experience of its workers, was able to be articulate about the limits of case work help for rent payment.

6. Angleshire

In Angleshire the formation of policy has a different history. No doubt because of its great size and the variety of different conditions within the county it has a tradition of issuing standing instructions as an administrative necessity. After the passing of the 1963 Act the power to give money was to rest with the children's department but consultations were to follow with the chief officers responsible for services concerned with the health and development of children and with senior officers of voluntary agencies and other statutory bodies operating in this field. As a result of these consultations the following principles of policy were announced, and were followed by standing instructions about what was available in the form of help:

Two kinds of application for material aid can be distinguished. In the first place, there are applications for grants which directly prevent the reception or retention in care of children, in circumstances in which families are not in chronic difficulties and there is unlikely to be a repetition of the request for aid. Examples are the payment of the railway fare of a girl living with her grandmother to enable her to return to the care of her mother, or the payment of the fare of a relative living at a distance to enable her to come to look after a family. Such requests may demand immediate consideration if the help is to be effective, but the decision will be a relatively simple one.

More difficult will be the larger class of applications in which the request for material aid for such matters as rent arrears, electricity and gas bills, food and bedding is a symptom of a chronic problem which will inevitably recur unless much time and skill is available to help the family sort out its difficulties.

It was suggested that such requests should be viewed in the light of manpower and skill,

otherwise the children's committee would simply be providing a form of 'relief' supplementing the work of the National Assistance Board and charitable organisations.

These principles were incorporated into standing instructions.

Material aid

Benefits in cash or kind are included as the local authority think fit, and therefore cannot be claimed as of right.

[Home Office circular No. 204/1963]

Material aid which may be provided by Areas under the Act falls into three categories:

(a) Grants for the general purposes of the Area under the Act, e.g. payment for the removal of furniture from a donor to the Area Office or elsewhere for storage.

(b) Grants for a specific purpose which directly prevents the reception or retention in care of children, in circumstances which are unlikely to be repeated. Examples are the payment of fares to enable a child to be returned to the care of his parents, or the fares of a relative living at a distance to enable her to come to look after a family.

(c) Grants or loans for such matters as rent arrears, electricity and gas bills, food and bedding.

The instructions stressed the fact that the new powers to give aid were not an alternative to National Assistance, and that the National Assistance Board (as it then was) should therefore be consulted before any assistance in cash or kind was given. The possibility of exploring charitable sources for grants was stressed. And material aid was to be confined to 'only essential items which are necessary to make a habitable home for the children'. The guide lines continue:

The payment of rent arrears or other sums due for services already received, such as gas, water or electricity bills, and hire-purchase debts, must be regarded as assistance in cash and as such may only be given in exceptional circumstances. When such help is recommended, consideration should be given to this being done in whole or in part by means of an interest free loan which the County Council would require to be repaid, if necessary, at a nominal rate which is within the financial scope of the family. Provision should be made for repayments to be waived if there is a deterioration in family circumstances. Such loans could assist in the payment of hire-purchase debts for essential items when it is clear that the family finances are in jeopardy because the rate at which debts were having to be repaid to creditors are far in excess of the family's ability to meet the demand and at the same time to meet its minimum day-to-day needs.

Consideration should be given, particularly in cases where there has been mismanagement of income, to the possibility of an initial minimum grant, the balance of the debt being repaid to the creditor at a rate agreed between the family, the case worker and the creditor.

Assistance should not normally be recommended towards the payment of hire-purchase debts for items such as television sets, radios, record players, cars, motor cycles or refrigerators. Generally, these items can be regarded as inessential and can be returned to the creditor.

It will be seen that the directions were explicit, and definite, and aid from the department was to be given only when other sources had failed. The pattern of delegation was also clearly delineated. A new sub-committee had been set up to deal with the new Act and new area sub-committees were formed. These last were empowered to authorise in any one year to any one family one grant, or recurring small grants, loans or gifts in kind up to a total of £50. These grants must then be reported to the county children's committee or the new central sub-committee, which alone had power to authorise sums of larger amounts. Emergency grants of up to £10 could be made on the advice of the area children's officer subject to the approval of the chairman of the area sub-committee; larger amounts required the approval of the county children's officer, the chairman of the children's committee and ratification by the children's committee or the central sub-committee. The county central office felt strongly that discretion should be exercised by lay committee members, and approved of the public accountability required of case workers when submitting cases for grants to them. Standing instructions were regarded as very valuable by the central administration because they were explicit, covering a majority of situations and ensuring that aid was used not by itself but as part of a case work plan. Such instructions were thought useful as a guide to which staff could turn when they were uncertain about giving money, and it was felt they helped workers to crystallise their thinking about the giving of financial and material help; it was therefore a valuable discipline to fulfil the requirements of the written instructions. It was thought, too, that clear instructions about the intention and practice of giving aid helped senior staff to be more confident in this new area of work. However, in practice the individual judgment of senior staff in each area seemed to be the major factor in deciding whether or not aid should be given in a particular case, although all staff worked within the broad intention of the standing instructions.

In the two county areas which we examined, the majority of grants and loans were, in fact, below £50, and, through making small grants, the case workers were able to involve the area sub-committee in their day-to-day work. Originally the idea was formed of giving loans rather than grants, since this practice was thought to be in line with county policy about giving money, but it also was felt that it maintained the self-respect of the client. In practice slightly more was spent on grants than on loans during the first three years, loans overtaking grants dramatically in the financial year 1966–67. Thereafter there was a complete reversal. Expenditure in the form of grants continued to rise while loans fell. However, the pattern varied in the two areas surveyed. The variations in Felcastle were greatest, and were due to a policy of using loans for clients to put down a deposit on a cheap house, and to provide a mortgage. The general development away from loans seems to have been due to the fact that the rate of recovery was so very poor, largely, it was thought, because the workers had not sufficiently taken into account the clients' other debts when expecting them to repay.

Looking at the county as a whole in the years of the research, 1966–68, the main item of expenditure, involving the biggest proportion of families, was arrears of rent or rates. Slightly more grants were given for this than loans. Gas and electricity bills were the second main items of expenditure, though not involving so many families. Although the majority of families receiving loans were helped with rent, gas or electricity arrears, this was not true of grants, many of which were small and were given for such things as household necessities and family emergencies. The type of help given is revealed in the sample of cases discussed later.

Owing to the high expenditure in the county for arrears of rent and rates, a rent guarantee scheme was introduced to limit these payments.

Material aid (which did not need the consent of the committee) was given by the county children's department chiefly in the form of second-hand clothing and furniture. The giving of second-hand goods was seen as a useful part of the case work plan where a client needed the experience of being given to, and such help was also considered expedient in some cases where families were large and the wear and tear on the furniture was extreme. In Colton, one of the two area offices involved in the research, such aid included the giving of Christmas presents and the lending of two second-hand electric kettles, useful when the gas had been turned off. In this area there was very little storage space in the office, and most of the second-hand goods were acquired from elsewhere—the WRVS, for example.

As in Milltown and Nordale, in Angleshire there was an ever-recurring need to take action about evictions. The county covers over 100 separate district housing authorities and a number of overspill areas. It is a reflection of the difficulties that arrangements to forestall evictions had been discussed with different housing authorities on and off since 1956. This discussion increased after 1963 and was intensified when the joint circular on *Homeless Families* was considered in 1966. The problem was 'a tendency for many housing authorities to leave referral too late and then expect the children's department to act as rent collectors. Many housing authorities do not appear to accept their welfare functions and expect the children's department to undertake this aspect of their work.' As the county council has the responsibility for all homeless families, the evictions of all the separate district housing authorities could constitute a serious problem. In 1967 district councils agreed in principle to a scheme under which they should refer to children's departments, at an early date, families with children likely to be evicted because of arrears. The county council would then guarantee to the district council the payment of rent.

The proposals stated:

If, in such circumstances, the social worker recommended that eviction be deferred and the recommendation was accepted by the district council, the county council would, in cases where children are involved, be prepared to indemnify the district council against further arrears in rent for an agreed period from the time at which the recommendation not to proceed with eviction was accepted. This indemnity would not cover arrears incurred up to that time, and any question of the payment of such arrears would have to be the subject of special consideration.

It is anticipated that in the majority of cases the necessity to call in a social worker would result from non-payment of rent. Although notification to the county council should be made at an early stage, the county council must look to county district councils to act with discretion in order to avoid social workers being swamped with cases of this kind, which would make it more difficult to deal effectively with those families where social case work might be of real value. The county council regard the prevention and collection of arrears as essentially part and parcel of normal housing management, and it would not be their intention that the practical effect of such arrangements should result in the social worker acting merely as a debt collector on behalf of the housing authority.

It was decided that rent should be indemnified for six months in the first instance and the children's department be responsible only for those arrears accrued during the period of indemnity. It was agreed that families should not be told that their rent was being guaranteed.

An area committee can give a rent guarantee for six months and then, since payments would normally have totalled £50, the case has to be referred to the county children's committee. In the event, the rent guarantee scheme has been very little used; the case workers in the children's departments in most areas have been collecting their clients' rent, regarding this as part of their case work in helping the client to cope. Rather the view was expressed that workers would like to see housing authorities more able to tolerate families who are experiencing difficulties and cannot cope effectively all the time with their numerous responsibilities. However, the introduction of the rent guarantee scheme served to involve the housing authorities in the problem. Its introduction did make it easier for housing authorities and children's departments to work together to prevent eviction.

The policy of Angleshire with regard to the employment of specialist workers in a specialised preventive section was different from both Milltown's and Nordale's. Angleshire, it is true, increased its staff substantially, employing family case workers who originally were supposed to have small case loads of twenty clients for intensive work, but the work of these family case workers and the work of the child care officers gradually merged, and by the time we interviewed the workers the distinction had ceased to exist. We shall see whether this difference in staffing policy had any effect upon the way aid was given. Of the two areas within the county which we examined, Colton, which covered an industrial redevelopment area and overspill estates, was the larger and had a high turnover of staff. The case loads ranged from thirty-six to fifty-six. Felcastle, more rural, a coastal area, less densely urbanised and more stable, had a lower turnover of staff, and, as work had not yet merged to the same extent, the staff involved in the study had smaller case loads. Both areas used consultation with senior staff as a major means of guidance about giving aid. In neither office did the case workers express any need for more specific guide lines to be laid down; they regarded each case as different, and whether aid was given or not depended upon the diagnosis and treatment plan, which worker and supervisor discussed together. The guide lines already laid down, though definite enough, were not generally felt to be too restricting, since they gave some room for flexibility at the area level.

In the central office of the county children's department there was a strong feeling that the exercise of discretion should be accountable to the committee members. The existing procedure for giving aid was favoured because the act of writing down facts and supervision at staff committee levels ensured a consideration of the effect financial aid was likely to have on the case work situation. This procedure also meant that the arguments put forward would be expressed clearly and unequivocally for presentation to lay members. It ensured that the giving of money to clients was considered from the point of view of the community as a whole (as represented by the committee) and not just from the case worker's standpoint. Further, it was argued that presenting cases to a committee made case workers examine whether there were more appropriate alternatives, e.g. that a client had made appropriate claims on the SBC. The practice of delegating powers from the central committee to the area committee was evolving, and area children's officers' powers to spend money in an emergency was increased from £1 to £2 at the beginning of 1969. They were also beginning to make more extensive use of their power to spend up to £10 in consultation with the area sub-committee chairman.

Senior staff in both areas examined each case very thoroughly, looking for other alternatives, before they would allow it to go forward to committee. Both areas drew considerably on the resources of charitable organisations before considering use of the children's department's funds. Though both areas helped the same number of cases, Colton obtained more than twice as much money in this way as Felcastle, which was an area with fewer local charities. However, most of the grants came from national charities or military funds, and were used as part of the case work plan and as support given to the family, not as a substitute for it. Interestingly enough, the two areas had quite different views about whether the county policy discouraged or encouraged the use of financial aid. In Felcastle it was felt that such aid was encouraged within the general context of preventing children coming into care. The senior staff were very clear about the kinds of problem in which departmental policy envisaged they would give financial aid—to help those prepared to use it to help themselves. In Colton the general feeling was different; it was thought that policy discouraged financial aid and indicated that it should be used only at the point of crisis. All workers, however, saw the aid being best given in the context of the imminent break-up of the family and the possible admission of children into care. There were some differences in the two areas in the strength of the officers' feelings about giving financial aid. In Colton there was a good deal more ambivalence than in Felcastle about whether it was the best form of help for the client. This may have been related to the different sort of office and staff; Colton was a busier office with a greater turnover of staff, and had the extra task of continually training new recruits who generally wanted to solve all problems at once and felt frustrated if they could not do so. This tended to produce some anti-paternalistic feelings about dispensing temporary financial aid.

We explored with the workers the kinds of situation in which they thought it inappropriate to give aid. In Felcastle the workers thought it was more constructive for the client to try and pay off the debts on his own without receiving aid, especially if there had been a history of getting into debt; they thought aid inappropriate if it had not helped in the past, or where there was no danger of the children being admitted into care. It was not thought appropriate for the children's department to help when other bodies, such as the Social Security office or the local education authority, had the primary responsibility. The answers in Colton were more varied but generally related to situations where, with support, families themselves could cope with debts (this was thought to preserve self-reliance) or where clients saw the department as a relief-giving body and were unable to accept case work help. Workers also included situations where there was sufficient money or where the client was endeavouring to extract money on false pretences. A minority of workers thought it inappropriate to give help where the family gambled, drank or squandered money.

All the officers in Felcastle, and the majority in Colton, were in favour of conditions being laid down, and the client knowing about them, when aid was given; for example, they felt clients must be clear that a loan should be repaid, or co-operation in case work expected if the rent was guaranteed by the children's department.

Although Angleshire was included in the research project as the only authority with written guide lines, in practice, as we have seen, these are no more than an expression of general policy which can be used for guidance in a difficult situation; the crucial factor governing whether aid was given or not was the assessment of the senior staff, particularly of the area officer. The children's department sees itself as a case work agency, and policy about financial aid is confined to general principles which are borne in mind when diagnosis and treatment might indicate its use. Here their practice was similar to that of the other departments we examined.

We can now begin to look at the sort of families, taken from the sample of cases, to which the workers gave financial or material aid because this sort of help was seen to be appropriate, and contrast this with families where such aid was not given.

In both Colton and Felcastle, although the areas were so different, certain similarities emerge. The reason why the department decided to give financial aid was the same in both cases—for specific housing situation. The number being helped with rent, rates or mortgage arrears was 58 per cent of cases in Colton and 50 per cent of cases in Felcastle. Next came aid for food, and afterwards for a variety of emergencies. Looking at the families receiving financial aid, the following characteristics were found. In Felcastle the majority of families (67 per cent) were married, with three children under 14 at home. In Colton just under half (43 per cent) were married, with three children under 18 at home. In both areas the majority of families were in accommodation rented from the local authority (86 per cent in Colton, 67 per cent in Felcastle), the majority in Felcastle and half in Colton having lived in the area for over five years. In Felcastle the majority of fathers (67 per cent) were unskilled manual workers. In Colton they were evenly divided between skilled and unskilled (36 per cent).

We next looked at the families' income, and here a problem arose, (see Appendix 1) as in 36 per cent of the families in Colton and 17 per cent of the families in Felcastle the income was not known. Where the income was known, 80 per cent of families were actually living at the subsistence rate; in Colton 56 per cent of families were on or below subsistence level. In Colton nearly half (43 per cent) of the families' income was from supplementary benefits; in Felcastle, a third (33 per cent). A minority of families relied upon the father's earnings—in Felcastle, only a small number (17 per cent); in Colton, just over a quarter (29 per cent). A large majority (86 per cent) in Colton had previously received case work

E

help from other agencies, and half only (50 per cent) in Felcastle. Where there were schoolchildren in the family some or all of the children were receiving free school meals in 50 per cent of the cases in Felcastle and 57 per cent of cases in Colton. As these are means-tested benefits, these figures confirm the level of poverty. Half the families in Felcastle had had children in care at some time, just over a third (36 per cent) in Colton, usually for short-term illness or confinement of the mother. An overwhelming number of families in both towns had never had a child appearing before the juvenile court.

The goals towards which worker and client worked with the use of financial aid were different in the two areas in the short term but similar in the long term. In Felcastle the main short-term goal was to ease housing problems (50 per cent), this was only the second immediate goal in Colton (43 per cent), improving the client's ability to cope and fulfil his parental responsibilities being the major aim (50 per cent). But this was the main long-term goal in both areas in the context within which financial help was given (100 per cent). Both areas felt they had been very successful in achieving their short term goals (93 per cent in Colton, 83 per cent in Felcastle). In the long term, in many cases, there had not been sufficient time to judge success. Felcastle was the more positive in outlook, seeing success in 50 per cent of the cases and failure in 33 per cent. In Colton 29 per cent of cases were seen as successful, with 36 per cent seen as failures. These figures seem to bear out the workers' fears that financial help in a crisis does not necessarily mean long-term success with their goal.

In the group of families where the help given was of a material kind, mainly second-hand clothing or furniture, generally no conditions were attached. In this group a very much larger proportion of families relied on the father's earnings (29 per cent in Felcastle, 42 per cent in Colton). This group was not so poor as the first group. Where the income was known, 40 per cent of families in Colton were at or below subsistence, and in Felcastle 33 per cent were at subsistence level, with no one below (see Appendix 3). In both areas a number of families had received help previously— more than half in Colton, and nearly a third in Felcastle. The large majority of recipients lived in council property. Again, the main long-term goal in both areas was helping parents fulfil their responsibilities, and in neither area were so many cases seen as unsuccessful (15 per cent in Colton, 14 per cent in Felcastle). In more cases the outcome was undetermined.

Those families receiving no aid at all in the preventive work in both areas were most likely to be dependent on father's earnings— 46 per cent of cases in Colton and 63 per cent in Felcastle. Questioning produced no clear answer as to why aid was not given, and revealed the complexity of motivation and assessment which lay behind the decision to give or not to give, and the differing influence of current area practice. It may be relevant as an indication of relative poverty in this group that there were fewer families with children receiving free school meals.

When we examined the purpose behind the help given in both the areas the main goal was always to help the family to function better and to fulfill its responsibilities. The housing management problem, though of great importance, was seen as only part of the task of family responsibility as a whole. The group which received financial aid had invariably the worst record of successful outcome in the long term, and this would seem to indicate the intractable nature of their problems and that the financial aid available to the department is quite ineffective by itself to enable the families to cope.

7. A Welsh county

The Welsh county, like the English county, consisted of distinct and different cultural regions—coastal, rural and industrial—and the children's department was divided into areas covering these different regions. Within the county were nearly a score of different housing authorities, ranging from those large enough to employ housing officers to those small enough for the treasurer to collect the rent. The children's department, though expanding at the time of our research, had a small nucleus of professional and administrative staff who had lived in the county for many years, and as a result there existed very good co-operation with other statutory and voluntary agencies concerned with the welfare of children and families. From the time of the formation of co-ordinating committees, after the issue of the joint circular in 1950, this co-operation had been extended and formalised in order to prevent the break-up of families. Since 1961 committees for families at risk had been formed in all the county areas, and the area officer in the industrial part of the county undertook a special period of work and training with the Family Service Unit to consolidate the preventive approach. Gifts in the form of second-hand clothing had been frequently given as part of the case work and, as in Milltown, small personal loans were made by workers to clients. Existing co-operation ensured that the housing authority in the industrial area informed the department of pending evictions, and personal contact between workers in the two departments meant that often there was agreement to suspend action while the children's department worked with the clients.

It will be seen that prior to the passing of the Children and Young Persons Act in 1963 a practice of preventive work and aid had been built up in certain limited and circumscribed ways based on experience and observation, ways which were then expanded and developed after 1963. Workers had case loads which covered the whole range of preventive and child care duties, and they were very large, consisting of 60 to 70 cases.

One of the immediate consequences of the 1963 Act was to increase the co-ordination already existing with various housing authorities. This was a direct result of the Home Office circular No. 204/1963 (see Appendix 2, paragraph 12). Following this circular, the deputy clerk organised two meetings of all the housing authorities in the county, and the children's department offered to help with problems on housing estates. It was stated in reply to our original questionnaire that, as a result of these two meetings:

Every housing authority now meets the children's department and other social workers concerned at a quarterly meeting. All inform us of mounting arrears as they are known, and we have free access to lists of tenants in arrears. Evictions now never take place without prior consultation and we are informed at the *latest*, when court action is intended.

The housing authority in the industrial borough where the main problems existed suggested that the county council should pay for housing welfare officers:

Staff on part loan were offered as an alternative, since they would have more ready access to county confidential records—health, juvenile courts, problem families, and cases in which the police were showing concern.

A child care officer was seconded for housing welfare and sat with the housing committee. One factor of concern to the committee was how to differentiate between a problem family (a concern of the children's department) and a problem tenant (a concern of the housing department). A problem tenant is not only someone who does not pay rent but may also be someone who is a disturbing neighbour, who is noisy or who does not keep the garden tidy. An important distinction was made here, but never clarified, as no clear differentiation between a problem family and a problem tenant was attempted, nor were the different natures of social work and housing management explored.

However, the practice of seconding a child care worker to the industrial town's housing department produced very successful results, although skilful diplomacy was necessary on the worker's part. When the worker left the county the secondment was discontinued because of the difficulty of coping with the politics involved in co-operation between the county authority and the non-county boroughs and urban and rural district councils responsible for housing.

In the more rural areas meetings to discuss the 1963 Act were called. Housing authorities, NSPCC, police, probation officers, chief health visitors, mental health and educational welfare officers who had families at risk, were all invited. In some cases the clerks and the treasurers came to discuss the problems of these families with the children's department. In this way informal education and co-operation developed between departments. The children's department asked the housing officers to inform them of tenants with families who were £10 in arrears with rent in order to discuss the question of 'who gives a short, sharp talk'. In fact, it was often just a matter of child care officers 'reading the Riot Act' on the assumption that some clients would realise the seriousness of the situation on being faced with the possibility that children might come into care. However, the children's officer recognised that in doing this the workers were exercising a discriminating technique of good housing management rather than case work skills.

There is close liaison with the county court bailiffs, who inform the children's department of problems arising from pending evictions by private landlords. Indeed, one of the big problems in rural districts is that of eviction from tied cottages, as obviously the department cannot be forewarned of these arrangements. However, no county court bailiff evicts without going to the children's department first; bailiffs even look for alternative accommodation. The department then visits and also helps the family to look for alternative accommodation.

The welfare department is responsible for Part III accommodation, which consists of two small flats a long and infrequent bus journey away from the biggest town in the county. In view of this the children's department later used the 1963 Act to extend accommodation. There are not many evictions and any evicted people usually go to relatives. Homeless families are allowed to stay in Part III accommodation for three months only.

However, the department has not admitted children into care because of eviction for a long time and, when it did so, the case was not only a problem of homelessness but was complicated by child neglect and the need to ensure the welfare of the children.

As a result of the close co-ordination with housing authorities a rent guarantee scheme was introduced. In fact the county council has made only four or five guarantees, and no money has ever been paid out. The value of the guarantee scheme has been that the child care workers visit the family on an intensive basis for a period of approximately one year, and give support and help with budgeting; it ensures, as far as possible, that the weekly rent is paid to the housing authority. Clients are not told when the rent is guaranteed. Under the 1963 Act annual provision was made in the estimates for £1,000 for financial aid in the first year, £860 in the second year and £1,000 again thereafter. However, in the first three years actual expenditure was only £241, £212 and £220. The department described its policy in the following words:

We do not pay debts for rent or services (gas, electricity, etc), but if there is good co-operation from the client, we will make a loan in emergency cases, i.e. no heat or light, imminent eviction. Grants would be discussed with the children's officer, but officers may make small grants for fares and food up to £2 and report back. This amount is to be increased. It would appear very necessary to keep grants to the minimum and avoid wherever possible a sapping of independence. We are under-staffed and emergency action becomes necessary too often.

We prefer guarantee payments or making a loan, as grants are easily abused. Occasionally emergency loans are found to have been given and they are replaced by outright grants when there is time to assess circumstances fully, i.e. we use all forms of aid and prefer them in the order of guarantee, loan, grant, for both economic and social reasons.

This reluctance to give money on the grounds that it will damage the self-responsibility and independence of the client is reflected in practice. Help is rarely given in the form of a cash payment. Where the client is in difficulties with a debt, the creditor is usually paid direct. Where there is a family crisis—usually because there is no money in the house for food—the client is normally given a voucher, in the form of a food order made out to a grocer who supplies the local children's home at a discount. The client is expected to reimburse the department for the food order, most orders being for sums of under £2. Of the orders we examined between 1967 and 1968, we found that about half had been repaid. One wonders whether the reasons put forward for not giving cash grants are really a rationalisation for economy, since the actual practical method of giving financial aid might seem more demoralising than a cash payment. However, clients were said never to have asked for money instead of the vouchers they were offered, and even to have preferred this method of payment, perhaps because they shared in the discount available.

The giving of aid in kind increased after 1963. A furniture store was set up and a delivery van provided so that second-hand furniture could be given. A small charge was made for both furniture and better clothing, as it was felt that clients preferred such a practice. However, workers tended to price the goods according to the needs and resources of the family, with no scale for comparison between workers. This sometimes made for difficulties when clients compared goods and prices with each other.

The store of second-hand clothing and furniture has expanded since 1963. The department gets a great deal of furniture—partly because senior staff know everybody in the area and also because staff regularly give talks to the Women's Institute and charities, who respond with gifts. Again, the workers' contact with the legal profession in custody cases has led to solicitors advising families of deceased people to let the children's department have furniture which is no longer required. In this way the children's department is able to clear whole houses of furniture and it is fortunate in having large outhouses in the grounds of the nursery which are used for storage. There is a magistrate, too, who runs a furniture firm, and when any reclaimed hire-purchase goods cannot be resold these are given to the children's department. Many prams are donated through contacts with the health visitor. Second-hand goods are also obtained from the surplus of rummage sales, and staff also organise coffee evenings to raise money to buy blankets. Indeed, all social agencies put into the store and take out of it. The supplementary benefit officers are often given help for families who are not known to the children's department. The turnover is rapid, since the policy of the department is very free as regards the giving of second-hand goods, although small charges are made where applicable. Behind all this work and co-operation is a desire not to spend more public money than necessary.

As the department was small and closely knit, and the children's officer was easily accessible, there was considered to be no real need to formalise delegation. The children's officer had power to approve payments, none of which has been over £10; the chairman and vice-chairman's consent was usually obtained before payment. and their action ratified by a special sub-committee of the children's committee. There was none of the formality required in the English county. If the children's officer was not available, and the crisis was urgent, the area officer would not hesitate to supply coal

or pay an electricity bill if, for example, children
in the winter months. At the time of our research
was growing, and additional senior staff were being
that more delegation was developing, along with
consultation and discussion. Appropriate charities
approached for large amounts of financial assistance;
charity had actually agreed to pay a bill of £82, thoug
cumstances here were regarded as rather exceptional.

Co-operation with the Social Security offices was good, a
been helped by the stability and experience of members of
in both departments. Because of this co-operation the county
developed an uncommon arrangement with the SB officers where
each paid half the arrears outstanding when it was decided to pa
a client's gas or electricity bill. The children's department's share
was in the form of a loan, which was of course always backed by
case work support for the family.

It will be seen that the workers' practice developed in the light
of day-to-day experience and professional consultation and supervision from senior officers. The judgment and personality of the
children's officer and the area officer of the industrial town were
very influential here. Though substantial provision was made in
the estimates for financial help, only about a fifth of the amount
estimated was in fact spent each year. The workers did not
experience any need for clearer guide lines to be laid down. The
only difficulty they experienced—and this we must regard as a
major one—was a need to clarify the distinction between the purpose of help given by the children's department and help given by
the SB officers. The *extent* to which help was given in the children's
department depended, in theory, upon the worker's case work
diagnosis and the future risk of neglect in the family, but the
workers' own feelings about dispensing money did play an important part in conditioning their decisions. On reflection, workers
considered that financial and material aid was best given in the
form of short-term loans, in a crisis, to a family in need where the
parents were good managers but had inadequate income, and that
it should be used only to prevent admission to care or neglect of
children, and only in cases where there was a possibility of the
family responding to the help and being enabled by it to cope better.
Therefore such help was not given to families where money was
badly managed and where help with budgeting was considered

ιore appropriate, or where a family was becoming dependent on he worker and had lost the will to help itself. Consideration was not given specifically to the therapeutic effect of financial aid to depressed clients.

The workers' ambivalence about giving at all was evident in the Welsh county, as in all the other regions we examined. It was frequently said, in relation to second-hand goods, that the act of giving was important, and established a relationship between worker and client. This point of view was not mentioned in regard to giving money, and indeed the request to the client for a small payment for second-hand goods—even to maintain the client's independence—might be seen as a contradiction or, at any rate, a sign of real ambivalence about giving aid at all. Workers were also concerned that they might become too responsible for having to ensure that the loans were repaid, and considered this was incompatible with their case work. Nor did their case work practice in general include helping the client to budget in detail, despite the emphasis which senior staff placed on this, and the fact that it was written into the terms of rent guarantees.

The department summed up its experience in regard to aid under Section 1 of the 1963 Act as follows:

The Act has helped us to round off our work. We are disappointed that rehabilitation has not reduced the numbers in care, but material aid is not the main factor affecting the breakup of family life. We are finding more evidence of unstable homes, rejected children, children and parents in need of psychiatric support or alternatively children in need of the neutral, stabilising background of residential care. Rehousing by authorities has been more rapid and more co-operative since our meetings started. Certainly a different attitude to eviction has grown since we have had opportunities to show that supportive action can save a large number of families being evicted. The housing authorities appear able to revise their attitudes if adequate social reasons supporting the welfare of the children are produced. We are all educating each other, in fact.

Our main problem is the totally inadequate accommodation for evicted families, and rehabilitative Part III accommodation has been closed down as unsuitable. There are very few 'half-way' houses available to the housing authorities, and the fact that a county authority is not a housing authority is a serious drawback.

To what sort of families was financial and material aid given? It is again clear from the sample of cases that the children's department was working with a group of families in real poverty. Looking at financial aid first, it was used to help families needing food in 41 per cent of the cases. Next came electricity arrears (29 per cent), clothing (18 per cent) and fares (12 per cent); the smallest amount of help was given equally for housing, paying a fine, for a gas meter and for coal (6 per cent). Financial help was given as a loan for the most part, though a significant percentage (12 per cent) of families received a straight grant, and most of the families (65 per cent) had received some sort of help previously. The families mainly consisted of three to five children living at home, and the vast majority, where the income was known, were living at or below a subsistence standard of living (see Appendix 3). Under half (41 per cent) were dependent on the father's earnings, and nearly half (47 per cent) were receiving a supplementary benefits allowance. Very few (6 per cent) were on the wage stop. The fathers were generally skilled (24 per cent) or unskilled (34 per cent) manual workers, though a sizeable proportion (18 per cent) were semi-skilled, and 18 per cent were agricultural workers. There were no cohabitations, the unions generally being legal marriages (65 per cent). In the remaining families, almost without exception, the mother was coping herself, alone and unsupported. Nearly three-quarters of the families (70 per cent) lived in accommodation rented from the local authority; almost all the rest, with the exception of a few in tied cottages, were in property rented from private landlords.

Just over half the families (59 per cent) had received help from other case work agencies in the past, chiefly from the NSPCC and the probation officers. The same number (59 per cent) were being helped by free school meals for all the children. More than half (53 per cent) had had a child in care in the past, and over a quarter (29 per cent) had a child who had appeared before the juvenile court. It can be seen, therefore, how linked with prevention of statutory care is the financial grant. The majority of families (41 per cent) in this group had been referred by the housing department; the next main sources of referral were the police (12 per cent) and the NSPCC (12 per cent). The financial help given was all below £25; the majority of it consisted of sums less than £5, and there was usually a condition to repay attached to receiving it.

When asked what were the reasons which prompted workers to give financial aid in the majority (77 per cent) of cases, they said it was done to maintain material standards in the home, such as heating, lighting or food required to prevent child neglect, or to help with a child care problem where money was needed to prevent neglect (35 per cent). Other reasons given were to ease the housing problem (12 per cent) or to help with a low-income situation (12 per cent). The short-term goals for which financial aid was used were: to improve the family's ability to cope with its responsibilities (47 per cent), prevent the break-up of the family (35 per cent), and ease the housing problem (41 per cent). Sometimes the grant enabled the worker to supervise or help the children more effectively (18 per cent). The overwhelming long-term goals were to strengthen parents' ability to cope with their responsibilities (71 per cent). Almost always (94 per cent) the workers felt they were successful in the short term. In the long term they felt there had not been sufficient time to judge (53 per cent), but nearly a third (29 per cent) of the cases were thought to be working out successfully. The significant factor in long-term success was not so much the financial help in itself but rather the support which the worker gave the client, so enabling him to take up a course of action he could not have managed alone.

In the second group of families, those which received second-hand goods or material aid, the majority (83 per cent) of families were married unions and only a small proportion (6 per cent) were unsupported mothers, compared with over a quarter (29 per cent) in the previous group. The majority of families had four or five children at home; over half these children (56 per cent) had been in care in the past, and a substantial proportion (22 per cent) had been before the juvenile court. A third of the families (33 per cent) were unskilled manual workers, 28 per cent semi-skilled and 11 per cent skilled; a very few (6 per cent) were agricultural workers. More than three-quarters of the families (78 per cent) lived in houses rented from the local authority, with a sizeable number (11 per cent) of houses being rented from private landlords. In this group many more families (66 per cent) were dependent upon the father's earnings and a much smaller proportion (17 per cent) were dependent upon supplementary benefits. Where the income was known, 31 per cent were at or below subsistence level (see Appendix 3). This sample of cases was mainly referred by the housing authorities (22 per cent), the health visitor (17 per cent), or were self-referred (22 per cent). The overwhelming reason for which material goods were given (67 per cent) was to maintain standards and ease a financial problem caused by low income; clothing and furniture were the main goods provided; both the short- and long-term goals were to help improve the family's ability to cope. In the majority of cases (78 per cent) the help achieved its object in the short term, but the assessment in the long run was less happy. Over a quarter of the cases (28 per cent) were unsuccessful and in over half (56 per cent) there had not been sufficient time to judge.

The group of families which received no financial or material help at all in the course of the department's preventive work gives a rather more independent picture. The majority relied upon the earnings of the father (57 per cent) or mother figure (11 per cent), and only a small proportion (5 per cent) upon supplementary benefits. The majority of fathers were semi-skilled manual workers (52 per cent) or unskilled manual workers (32 per cent), with a smaller proportion of skilled men (11 per cent). Only 16 per cent of these families had had children in care during the past, and very few (5 per cent) had children who had appeared before a juvenile court. Without exception these families were all council tenants. In working with these families the increase of their ability to cope was, as elswhere, a major short-term goal (58 per cent) and the chief long-term goal (53 per cent), but, as in the first group which received financial help, help with a housing problem (53 per cent) was ranked almost as high. The case work help was seen as overwhelmingly successful (95 per cent) in the short term, and less so (16 per cent) in the long term.

It is clear as far as the Welsh county is concerned that in the short term the importance of using financial aid at the right time can be an important element in success. In every instance and group, however, the most important factor in success was thought to be the support of the worker rather than the financial or material aid. Financial aid was clearly linked to poverty and unemployment. However, the group which received material aid, even though it was economically better off than those who received financial aid, had the highest long-term failure rate. We could only speculate about the reasons for this.

8. Conclusions

We undertook this study because there was a good deal of concern and confusion in children's departments about the giving of financial aid. This concern was natural, despite the limitations set by Section 1 of the Children and Young Persons Act and the guidance offered in the Home Office memorandum, since many social workers and social administrators had no previous experience or theory to guide them about dispensing money.

The Home Office memorandum on the Act stated that Section 1

does not give power to intervene in family difficulties or domestic problems unless there is some reason to suppose that this may create the risk of children having to be received into or committed to the care of the local authority, nor does it give power in any circumstances to impose guidance on parents who are not willing to receive it. [Paragraph 8]

Financial or material help, therefore, must clearly be part of a case work plan in which parents co-operate to prevent the children being received into the care of the local authority or committed by the court. Because case work is so specifically individualised the giving of such help within the overall plan *must* be discretionary and not subject to eligibility rules. Here is an example (given to us by a worker in a Family Welfare Association) showing the advantage of a social work agency having discretionary power to give aid at the appropriate moment:

. . . Let me give you an illustration of a family with two young children and parents in their 20's. Father had a steady job and income. He undertook to buy a small house, had to furnish it, so he committed himself to HP. He became sick with an ulcer, was off work for months. His debts mounted. He felt hopeless. He became increasingly paralysed by feelings of inadequacy and so quite incapable of looking at his difficulties. The mortgagor's warnings provoked no real action other than that of apparent indifference and irresponsibility. Likewise electricity bills and rates demands. The furniture was repossessed. The father felt more guilty and became more paralysed. A third child was born. A health visitor contacted an agency. Could we get the electricity on for the sake of this third child, who was currently in hospital? When the case worker visited, he found this paralytic, irresponsible father making inappropriate schemes, agreeing over-readily to suggestions from the case worker and then not acting on them. The father was physically almost ready to return to work but so overwhelmed by the difficulties that he was not really able to regard this as very hopeful and constructive. The case worker, after deliberation, decided not to seek financial help at this stage, since the cost of getting the electricity on might be the further depression of the father and so might not help in the long run. The family case worker decided to play for higher stakes first. He returned to the father and talked with him about his feelings at being off work for so long, at not being able adequately to care for his family, at seeing their conditions deteriorate, at being hounded by creditors, at being helpless. The father's reaction was much warmer, less guarded. He responded to this approach to the essential man in an almost impossible situation through little fault of his own. In a short while he returned to work, emotionally supported through the difficult first three weeks before he drew a full week's wages. Meanwhile he was able to adopt a much more positive approach to his financial difficulties, and in view of this and the fact that the new-born baby was coming home, the case worker sought a grant to enable the electricity supply to be reconnected. The committee sanctioned it and the family was much encouraged. The outlook was much more promising. Clearly, there is a great advantage in aid and case work coming from the same source and not really being available to the client as a right—in those circumstances where there are the special kinds of needs that I have been discussing.

Nevertheless, it was the absence of precise eligibility rules, the apparent arbitrariness of decisions, the responsible nature of public accountability, the stigma imposed by society upon their particular clients, the history of charity as opposed to rights, and additional feelings about giving or withholding money, which made the problem so acute for the workers. They were engaged in an exercise illustrating the classic dilemma and dynamism of social work (too seldom acknowledged): how to meet the needs of individual clients within the structure and framework of a social policy which must also be determined by the resources of money, skill and knowledge available at any time. These needs and resources are held in tension while the client is helped, but the dilemma itself goads social workers to contribute to the development of social policy and so to lead forward into social change.

Our local study of the kinds of families who were helped, the kind of help given, and our very tentative assessment of its effectiveness, served to underline some general facts we know from the national statistics. We found, for example, throughout the region a wide variation in the areas between the expenditure (as much as between £0·7 and £18 in the amount spent per thousand of the population under 16, for example) and an overall increase in the amounts given during the period 1964–69. Reports from the Advisory Council on Child Care show that financial and material help given by children's departments increased substantially during this period, even taking into account the fall in the value of money. The rate of increase of cash assistance has been about £58,000 per year, rising from £88,000 in 1966 to £202,900 in 1969—an increase of 200 per cent, mainly in expenditure on rent, domestic services and household requirements. Although the pattern differs from authority to authority, there is some evidence of a national trend towards more help being given in the form of loans. In our study, however, a pattern of loans gave way to a pattern of grants. There is also evidence in our study of the way in which not only the amount but also the manner in which cash assistance was given was determined, as far as help with rents went, by local housing problems and policies in the first instance, and subsequently modified by the local practice of the child care workers and the response of the clients to the help they offered. Nordale was perhaps the clearest example of this, though each area showed a sensitive modification in the light of the local situation. In contrast, our study also showed the reluctance of local children's departments to indemnify public utilities. Even though families incurred debts because their gas and electricity bills were unpaid it was not usual for grants or loans to be given for the purpose of clearing these debts.

More important, our study brought to life the encounter between families with problems and the social workers' use of financial and material aid in supporting them. We studied how the workers responded to the challenge of this, and saw how their response in turn influenced the development of new policies.[1]

The two major purposes of using financial aid were found to be, first, to keep families in their home, and second, to provide food in emergencies. All the departments in our study used their new

---

[1] The case studies in *Social Policy and Administration* by D. V. Donnison and V. Chapman (Allen & Unwin, 1965)—particularly the one of a change in policy initiated in an area office of a children's department—describe and analyse this same process.

powers under the Children and Young Persons Act to ensure the provision of a house for families needing one, seeing this as the first step in prevention, insuring their clients against eviction and homelessness, which drastically disrupt family life. Because so many of the families were the concern of the housing committee and were already in council houses, the children's departments' powers largely took the form, in our study, of indemnifying the housing committee against loss through families who were not paying their rent.[2] Alternatively, we have seen that one local authority had earlier allowed its children's committee to acquire property of its own which the department could then re-let as a preventive measure. This housing welfare function was temporarily taken over by children's departments as part of their work to ensure the prevention of neglect, but, except in Angleshire, this did not involve the most frequent form of expenditure under the Act, and, as we have seen, it was found that the case work support and help of the child care workers was an important factor in enabling the rent to be paid. The most frequent form of financial aid was used as a crisis response and was a grant or loan for food in all the areas, except Angleshire, where the main expenditure was on grants or loans to cover rent. The special problems of Angleshire in the field of housing welfare have, however, already been mentioned.

A further very important fact which emerged from our study was that many social workers believed that dealing in cash confused their role and had no positive contribution to make to their case work. This was a very real concern to them, and was revealed to our researcher in the discussion about giving and withholding money and the budgeting involved in the rent guarantee scheme. Emphasis on budgeting was actually written into the guarantee scheme in the Welsh county, but was implicit in the work of all the other departments we examined. However, when the child care workers were interviewed the majority said they did not help clients with budgeting in detail, but only in the ordering of priorities for spending. A minority of older workers saw budgeting as a positive way of helping the clients. The majority, however, mainly young workers, expressed hopelessness about enabling a family to budget on a low income. Some were upset at the prospect of budgeting for clients because they themselves had no need to do

---

[2] In the pilot study, however, grants were preferred for this purpose and were more typical of the region.

F

this on their own income. In interviews with the workers our researcher examined the problems they themselves experienced around the power to give or withhold financial aid and the necessity to collect money and debts from clients. There was a wide range of feeling. Some said they had no problems at all; at the other extreme were those who wished the department did not have this arbitrary power. The most problematic area was that of collecting loans made by their own department and, perhaps because of this, we found loans were collected haphazardly on the whole. When money had to be refused, workers almost invariably offered some alternative help, such as referral to another agency, or offered a different solution to the problem. On the rare occasions when neither alternative was open, workers expressed feelings of real distress and fell back upon departmental policy about giving money. A clear-cut direction—for example, that no grants are given at all—seemed more supportive to the worker in that it absolved him from having to exercise arbitrary power.

Giving aid did not evoke as much feeling as withholding it, but there were marked variations between workers as to whether the giving of aid was good or bad for the client. Workers were aware that their feelings could sometimes affect their decision about what kind of help it was appropriate to offer. The discussion of this whole subject was often painful to the workers and we appreciated the self-insight and openness which they shared with our research worker.

This view about the confusion of role is startlingly corroborated in the study made recently by Martin Davies on the association of probation officers with the payment of court fines owed by their clients.[3] This research shows clearly that difficulties arise when the probation officer is himself involved in the task of fine retrieval, and that it is doubtful whether the probation officer can successfully combine a helping role with that of specific mediator or debt collector. Although the position is even more acute for probation officers, in that they are clearly seen by the client to be servants of the court, the finding that the task of chasing defaulters is a time-consuming one, with little or no positive case work content, adversely affecting the client–worker relationship in about a fifth of the cases, is clearly relevant to our own study—particularly when

[3] *Financial Penalties and Probation*, a Home Office Research Unit report, HMSO, 1970.

we remember that in the majority of the cases the child care workers themselves said that their support and encouragement of the family through primary focus on case work were more significant in enabling the rent to be paid than the guarantee of cash assistance.

Our study describes the practice of the social workers in children's departments faced with their new powers to dispense money and various forms of financial aid. We see the work being done in the context of the 1963 Children and Young Persons Act, which gave the focus of child care another dimension. Historically the social services for children have been concerned to *protect* them from a hostile environment, from disease and death, and from cruelty and neglect. The 1963 Act effectively moved the focus of the service upon the prevention of family break-up, and this determined the goal which the workers set before themselves. In our studies the long-term goals of case work involving financial aid were always to enable the parents to cope properly with their parental task. (This was the goal of 72 per cent of the cases in Milltown, 80 per cent in Nordale, 100 per cent in Felcastle and Colton, and 71 per cent in the Welsh county.) These long-term case work goals were seen to be determined by the principle embodied in the relevant legislation. Short-term goals were invariably linked to the long-term aim of enabling the parents to cope, and in every case some easing of the housing problem was part of working towards this goal. In the short term the clients who received financial aid achieved the goal in the vast majority of cases (92 per cent)—this varied between 80 per cent (Nordale) and 100 per cent (Milltown)—but in the long term the goal was harder to achieve and the success rate averaged only 35 per cent (ranging between 29 per cent in the Welsh county and 40 per cent in Nordale). It seems clear from this that immediate financial aid is effective help in family crisis situations and that deliberate liaison with housing departments and informed housing management is an important aspect of preventive social work in a crisis. But, in the long term, the complexities of human problems are greater than the skill of social workers to amend, whether financial aid is given or not. The child care workers had raised their goal beyond the immediate prevention of family break-up in a crisis to the promotion of good parenthood, and it would seem that this may not be a realistic goal for some of the families. Perhaps it must be squarely faced that, in

the majority of cases in child care, realistic goals are skilled support and help—including financial help—through the continuing
crisis of family life until the children are independent. This is
indicated by the large number of families where the results of case
work were not known—not sufficient time to tell—and points to
the need for future research into differentiating those families for
whom these different goals are realistic, and perhaps considering the different roles of local authority and voluntary social
services.[4]

We have seen that the social workers' main task was to assess
the situation and whether it would be appropriate to use their new
powers to help the client in the light of their goal. The way they
approached the problem was influenced by local situations, particularly by the local housing management policies or lack of them.
The circular of guidance issued by the Home Office after the passing of the 1963 Act, to which we have frequently referred (see
Appendix 2), made reference in paragraph 12 to the possibility of
contribution towards the expenses incurred by housing authorities
and the prevention of eviction, but the children's committees each
developed their own form of liaison which was intended to be of
mutual benefit to each department, as well as to help the families
to keep their homes and cope with their family responsibilities.
Following this, the workers had to decide in which cases help
should be given. In social work this is a very old question. At one
time it took the form of distinctions between the 'deserving' and
the 'undeserving' poor, with overtones of moral judgments about
the undeserving who did not respond to social pressures. We chose
to ask the workers when they considered financial help was *appropriate*; their answers reflected what the joint wisdom of the department considered appropriate as a result of its experiences.

They showed that the assessments of appropriateness were
strongly influenced by the experiences of senior staff and their
interpretation of the Act. Grants, loans or guarantees were given
where there were large families; where there was a possibility of
collecting a loan back because the client was responsive to case
work help; where there was no alternative accommodation; where
families had severe physical or mental handicaps; where there was
no other means of preventing the children coming into care; where

---

[4] I.e. local authorities having powers—and duties—to do effective crisis
work.

the cost of children coming into care would be saved; where families were really trying to help themselves; where the family was in a crisis in imminent danger of disintegration; where parents were good managers. These were the conditions where help was thought appropriate. Were the workers right? In the short term they were. In the long term it is impossible to tell, but, on the whole, workers felt that their limited financial aid was less effective than their supportive case work. Workers were clearly haunted and troubled by the old spectre of the 'deserving' and the 'undeserving' poor, and their insecurity really came from being faced with clients in desperate need.[5] Workers wanted to help them all financially but were unable to justify doing so, particularly in the long run, because they knew that financial help *by itself* would not guarantee that they would achieve the goal.

What recommendations can be made from this research, this description of the way some local children's departments operated? We see departments tackling a new dimension of work. How did they set about establishing policies? What factors were important in modifying the policies in the light of the field workers' experience?

First, we saw the importance of good internal communication within the departments. The support and guidance of senior staff were very effective in enabling workers to come to decisions, and there was machinery for discussion, consultation and approval at all levels in all the departments. This was important in sustaining the morale of workers in a difficult job, and enabling them to think through the effect of what they were doing.

Second, we saw the need for co-operation and mutual understanding between the children's department and outside agencies. The *effective* giving of financial and material aid within the context of the Act was dependent upon the mutual understanding of the different roles of the child care workers and officers of the housing department, Social Security and so on. Where this understanding was good they were able to develop complementary policies, bearing the other agencies in mind. This made for more

---

[5] In Appendix 3 we have drawn together all the information we were able to obtain about the financial circumstances of the families helped. In all areas the great majority of those in Group 1 were living on or below the supplementary benefits 'subsistence level' scale. Appendix 3 also shows that the factors which distinguished the three groups were source of income, amount of income, type of work, and whether the children had been in care.

effective support for the client and a more economical organisation of joint resources.

Third, we see the need for the social workers continually to be aware of what they are doing, to take stock and consider where their policies are taking them. This, as we have seen, can lead to the development of change within the services arising out of the 'grass roots' experience of the workers and the continual monitoring of the effect of their work.

Finally, we see a need to face the dilemma of social work—reconciling needs and resources—and to think through the role of the social worker. By its very nature it must be a role of uncertainty, stress and change, and workers have to find their own ways of dealing with the anxieties consequent upon this. But the dilemma has an inherent dynamism which makes it impossible for social work to stand still while services develop and legislators legislate. Social work seems inseparable from the development of changing policies based upon people's needs.

This study will have served its purpose if it does no more than increase awareness of the positive contribution which social workers can make to the development of changing policies even while—or, indeed, just because—they spend most of their time helping individual families with their complex and often seemingly intractable problems. Social workers operate at the retail end of the social service business. Theirs is a face-to-face contact with the consumer and they have no escape from the harsh reality of the client's present problems. How they use their resources of time, skill and now financial and material aid to help solve or alleviate them, and what information they pass back to the wholesalers (the planners and administrators), will determine the extent to which changing policies in the personal social services are going to reflect a more realistic assessment of need and a more effective use of resources, today and tomorrow.

Appendix 1. Methodology

Initially a questionnaire was sent out to all the sponsoring local authorities, while a pilot study was carried out in an area of a large county borough, mainly to determine three things. First, to test a questionnaire to be applied to a sample of current cases; second, the form of interviews to be undertaken with field workers; lastly, what areas of departmental practice needed to be considered.

In view of the rapid staff turnover and the limitations of case work records, the research was focused on current cases, dividing them into groups to reveal the characteristics of families receiving aid. On a specified date field workers were asked to put all their *preventive* cases on a list (in no particular order), dividing them into four groups. Group 1 included those families that had received financial aid (i.e. grant, loan or guarantee). Group 2 were families that had received material aid only at no direct cost to the department. Group 3 were families that had received neither financial nor material aid. Also listed were current rehabilitative cases involving financial aid (group 4).

In the pilot study the children's department did not divide the field work, with some staff specialising on preventive work while others concentrated on the traditional departmental work. A sample of cases was chosen by the researcher as randomly as possible but weighted to get a fair sample in each group. This was revised in the main study, as detailed later. Very few current cases were listed in group 4, so to increase the numbers some closed cases were chosen. This was abandoned in the main study. In this way the following sample was obtained:

		Total	Sample
Group 1		39	30
2		26	25
3		104	40
4 :	current	6	
	closed	12	18

The sample was influenced by the researcher's decision to limit the number of questionnaires to a maximum of ten cases per field worker. This proved to be too many, as the questionnaires were long and complex. Staff were asked to complete the questionnaires in respect of the circumstances of families in the sample on 31 July 1967.

Meanwhile the areas for the main study were chosen as described in Chapter 1. The field workers were asked to list any current cases on a specified date coming under four headings, as in the pilot. The researcher then chose the sample, limiting the number of questionnaires to a maximum of eight per worker. Choosing the sample was simplified by taking the first two cases from under each group heading on each field worker's list. Where this fell short of eight, additional cases were included by taking the last case in the most heavily weighted group. This was necessary as two county boroughs chosen for the main study (Milltown and Nordale) had specialist sections for preventive work. Virtually the total case loads of the latter came into the study. Therefore some child care officers from the other section had only one or two preventive cases. Hence the wide variation in the totals in the table below. The Welsh county did not have a specialist preventive section, most field workers having mixed case loads. The department was small enough for the whole county to be involved in the research. As Angleshire children's department was much larger, it was decided to examine two contrasting area offices, Colton and Felcastle. Colton area office covered a number of urban districts and overspill estates but the Felcastle office covered urban, rural and coastal districts. Originally this county had specialised the work into preventive and traditional functions, but was in the process of merging case loads to encourage more emphasis on rehabilitation. This process was almost complete in the larger office, Colton, and fifteen field workers were involved in completing questionnaires, nine of whom had six or more cases in the study. In contrast, Felcastle was much smaller and still largely specialised, so that only five field workers were involved in the study, and two of these had only one preventive case. The proportion of preventive cases receiving financial aid in the two areas contrasted dramatically, as seen in Table 1. The limitations described above resulted in small samples in some areas. This resulted in the numbers shown in Table 1.

The field workers were given the sample of families and asked to complete questionnaires in respect of the families circumstances

Table 1

	Milltown		Nordale		Welsh county		Anglieshire Colton		Felcastle	
Group	Total	Sample	Total	Sample	Total	Sample	Total	Sample	Total	Sample
1	62	18	17	10	46	17	16	14	19	6
2	41	15	26	17	43	18	47	26	8	7
3	41	15	17	16	41	19	61	31	10	8
4	1	1	5	4	8	5	5	5	1	1

on 14 June 1968. The questionnaires contained amendments based on experience gained in the pilot study.

In all departments very few cases fell into group 4, as rehabilitation was universally interpreted as meaning children in care but home on trial, or children being actively rehabilitated. Apparently very few such current cases involved financial aid. However, the three preventive groups all included some families where one or more children had been in care in the past or even were currently in care. The main analysis is therefore based on these three groups.

Personal interviews were held with field workers who had completed questionnaires. An interview sheet of open-ended questions was used, designed to test staff attitudes towards departmental policy and to obtain information about workers' own practice and their feelings about the power to give or refuse financial or material aid.

Interviews with senior staff were less structured. Committee members were not interviewed. Committee minutes, records of expenditure, loan repayments and referral records were consulted. Separate reports were compiled for each of the departments involved in the study.

G

Appendix 2. Home Office circular No. 204/1963

Section 1 of the Children and Young Persons Act, 1963

Extension of powers of local authorities to promote welfare of children

1. I am directed by the Secretary of State to say that he proposes to bring into operation on 1 October 1963 Section 1 of the Children and Young Persons Act, 1963, which extends the power and duty of local authorities to promote the welfare of children. Detailed notes on its provisions will be found in the Appendix to this circular.

2. County councils and county borough councils, as local health, welfare, education and children authorities, already undertake much preventive work. The importance of Section 1 is that it confirms and significantly extends their power and duty to take action to prevent or remove conditions that may result in children coming into or remaining in care or being brought before a juvenile court, whether as offenders or as in need of care or protection. The Secretary of State believes that the progress made by local authorities with the remedial aspects of child care since the war must now be matched by progress in preventive action. He is confident that the effort required to achieve such progress will be repaid by the saving in suffering and insecurity to the children themselves, by the saving to the community in crime and maladjustment among its future citizens and by savings in the cost of the child care service itself.

3. It was emphasised in the Home Office circular (No. 160/1948) on the Children Act, 1948 (which related only to children deprived of a normal home life), that it was important to do everything possible to save children from suffering this misfortune, that it must be the first aim to keep the family together, and that the separation of a child from its parents could be justified only when there was no possibility of securing adequate care for a child in his own home. In July 1950 the Home Office, Ministry of Health and Ministry of Education issued a joint circular to local authorities inviting their attention to the need to co-ordinate the statutory and voluntary services concerned with the welfare of families and

children in order to deal effectively with the problem of children neglected or ill-treated in their own homes. Most county and county borough councils have now made co-ordinating arrangements.

4. It is not the intention of Section 1 of the 1963 Act to supersede the arrangements made since 1948 for the performance and co-ordination of preventive work. But in their welfare work with families where Children are likely to need care, local authorities have felt the need for express statutory authority to perform such work and to meet any consequent expenditure. Section 1 provides this authority.

5. Hitherto there has been no statutory focus of responsibility for ensuring that action was taken to give timely and effective help in family situations which were deteriorating to a point at which the children were at risk of having to be received into care or committed to care by a court. This responsibility will now rest on the council as the children authority. It will be their duty to ensure that the necessary advice, guidance or assistance is provided, both generally and in particular cases, either directly through one or other of their own services or indirectly through a voluntary organisation.

6. In some cases it may be possible for the help required to be given by the children's department; in others again, all the help necessary may be available from other services of the local authority or from voluntary organisations, so that no direct action by the children's department itself is required. Section 1 of the Act will not disturb existing arrangements which are working satisfactorily nor will it confer a monopoly of preventive work upon children's committees or their staffs. There is nothing to prevent arrangements being made in the future between the children's committee and other committees for preventive work to be done by the staff of other departments. Indeed there is everything to commend this from the point of view of the most efficient use of trained staff. The Secretary of State and the other Ministers concerned hope that in practice the work will be done by the officers of whichever service may be most suitable in a particular case and that full use will be made of those preventive services which already exist wherever their help can be effectively enlisted for the assistance of families in difficulty.

7. Section 1 has been drawn in sufficiently wide terms to give scope for initiative and experiment by local authorities (but it will be noted that assistance in cash is to be given only in exceptional

circumstances). The Secretary of State does not think it would be appropriate for him to attempt to list the range of possible activities; but there are some particular aspects of the work on which authorities might welcome advice.

8. *Limitation of the new powers.* The section does not give power to intervene in family difficulties or domestic problems unless there is some reason to suppose that these may create a risk of children having to be received into or committed to the care of a local authority. Nor does it give power in any circumstances to impose guidance on parents who are not willing to receive it.

9. Although the object of the new provisions is to reduce the need to receive or keep children in care, reception into care may of itself sometimes have a certain preventive value. The reception into care of one or more of the children for a period may enable a family to cope better with its other children, and thus preserve a home to which the former child or children may eventually return.

10. *Liaison with National Assistance Board.* It is not intended that the power to give material assistance under Section 1 of the Act should be used to provide an alternative to National Assistance or a child care supplement to National Assistance payments—continuing payments would in any event have to be taken into account as a resource by the Board in deciding the amount of a regular National Assistance grant. It will therefore be necessary for the authority to arrange for close liaison with the National Assistance Board to ensure that assistance, whether in kind or in cash, is not given in circumstances where it could more appropriately be given by the Board or where the result would be an unjustifiable duplication of expenditure from public funds. Except in cases of emergency where the assistance, if it is to serve any useful purpose, must be given at once, the Board should be consulted before any assistance in cash or in kind is given. Where the head of a household is in full-time employment the Board's powers to give assistance are extremely limited, and in such cases there will ordinarily be no need for the authority to consult with the Board.

11. It may sometimes be appropriate that assistance in cash should be given not outright but by way of a loan which the authority would subsequently require to be repaid.

12. *Liaison with housing authority.* A circumstance which may result in children being received into care is eviction, whether due to the ordinary termination of a tenancy or to the failure of the

parents to pay rent or to keep other conditions of the tenancy. Some of the problems arising in this way are dealt with in the Ministry of Housing and Local Government and Ministry of Health joint circular on homeless families, issued in March 1959. It will be open to the council under Section 1 of the new Act to make contributions towards the expenses incurred by housing authorities in providing accommodation for such families, as well as to provide services which may help to prevent eviction.

13. *Liaison with voluntary organisations.* The Secretary of State hopes that the council will maintain close liaison with voluntary organisations in their area active in the field with which this section of the Act is concerned. Local authorities will have discretion under sub-section (2) of Section 1 of the Act to make arrangements for voluntary organisations to give advice, guidance and assistance on their behalf. Such arrangements may be made either generally or in particular cases, but the authority will need to satisfy themselves that the arrangements ensure the adequate discharge of their duties under Section 1 of the Act in the field to which the arrangements apply. The arrangements may include contributions to voluntary organisations in respect of additional expenditure incurred by them on such preventive work. Such contributions need not be confined to direct payments for material necessities or case work services provided by a voluntary organisation; for example, a payment might be made to a voluntary organisation to meet the cost of transporting and storing furniture given by the general public to help families in difficulties. Many voluntary organisations which are not directly concerned with the care of children may also be able to help with preventive and rehabilitative work.

14. *Liaison with social welfare charities.* Section 12 of the Charities Act, 1960, provides for co-ordinating the activities of the council and those of charities established for purposes similar or complementary to the services provided by the council, in the interests of persons who may benefit from those services or from the charity. It also gives authority for the mutual disclosure of information in the interests of the beneficiaries. The Secretary of States hopes that councils and charity trustees will take advantage of these provisions. In particular, it may be found that trustees of a local charity for the benefit, for example, of the poor or of the sick, may be able and willing to provide additional benefits in cash or kind to meet a particular requirement of the family, if the circum-

stances are brought to their notice. The Charity Commissioners have indicated that, in their view, it would be proper for the trustees of such charities, if they wish, to apply their resources in this way to prevent hardship or distress. The indexes of local charities which are now being distributed to local authorities by the Charity Commissioners under Section 10 of the Charities Act, 1960, will, it is hoped, provide useful information regarding the charitable benefits available and the addresses of the persons administering them.

15. *Liaison with the Churches.* Section 1 of the Act should widen the scope for fruitful co-operation with the clergy and congregations of the various denominations in work contributing to the welfare of children. Much has already been done to bring to the notice of Church members the need to secure more foster parents and to befriend children and staff in residential homes for children; there should be an even wider range of possible work open when Section 1 comes into force. It might make for easier communication with Church members if your authority were to invite local Churches, or, where they exist, local councils of Churches, to nominate representatives, for purposes of consultation, who have knowledge of the statutory social services and of Church members willing and able to help. Where a local council of Churches comprises representatives of the Anglican and Free Churches only, an independent approach to the Roman Catholic and Jewish communities may be necessary.

16. *Provision of advice; family advice centres.* The Committee on Children and Young Persons (the Ingleby Committee) examined the possibility of creating in the large local authority areas a 'family advice centre' which would serve as a central point of reference for members of the public who were in need of advice or assistance on the welfare of children. The Secretary of State hopes that your authority will give further consideration to the possibility of such a point of reference for members of the public, since it is important not only that advice and assistance should be available, but that it should be known to be available, and that those who are in need of help and advice may be encouraged to seek it and may be enabled to discover where it can be obtained. It is not suggested, however, that it should invariably be necessary, even in the larger local authorities, to establish separate 'advice centres'. It may be possible to arrange—by the attendance of social case workers at certain times—for help to be given by existing Citizens' Advice

Bureaux, or for existing local authority offices—such as area offices of children's departments—to be ready to offer advice on family problems. Such centres will also be of value in assisting families or individuals where no question arises of children going into care and where indeed no children may be involved.

17. A further communication will be sent to you in due course about the reports to be made in accordance with sub-section (4) of Section 1 of the Act.

18. Additional copies of this circular are enclosed for the information of the Children's Officer, the Medical Officer of Health, the Chief Welfare Officer, the Education Officer and the Financial Officer. Copies have also been sent to the Clerks and Medical Officers of Health of authorities exercising delegated health and welfare functions.

Appendix

1. Under sub-section (1) of Section 1 a duty is laid upon local authorities to make available such advice, guidance and assistance as may promote the welfare of children (who are defined under sub-section (5) as persons under the age of 18) by diminishing the need to receive them into, or keep them in care, or to bring them before a juvenile court. The provisions which are made to discharge this duty may, if the local authority thinks fit, include provision for giving assistance in kind or, in exceptional circumstances, in cash.

2. Sub-section (1) of Section 1 of the Act refers to diminishing the need to keep children in care as well as to preventing their coming into care, and the duty which it imposes and the powers it confers apply equally to the rehabilitation of families whose children are already in care.

3. The duty is to make advice, guidance and assistance 'available'; there is no power to compel the acceptance of these services. Benefits in kind or in cash are included as the local authority think fit and therefore cannot be claimed as of right.

4. The provision of guidance would cover the training of problem families in household management and the provision of accommodation for that purpose. It is not, however, intended that the arrangements some authorities have made under existing powers, to provide special accommodation for the purpose of rehabilitation what are sometimes described as 'problem families', should be

duplicated under the new powers or that the responsibility of welfare authorities for assisting families of this type in temporary accommodation should be in any way diminished.

5. The power to give assistance in kind will enable household necessities such as bedding, kitchen equipment and fuel to be provided for families who are in immediate need of such assistance if they are to have a habitable home for their children. The fact that such assistance may involve the payment of money to someone else for the goods which a local authority makes available to the person assisted does not mean that such assistance is to be regarded as assistance in cash. The payment of money directly to the person assisted is assistance in cash, and under Section 1 may be made only in exceptional circumstances. The payment of rent arrears or other sums due for services already received, such as gas, water or electricity bills, should be regarded as assistance in cash.

6. By virtue of paragraph 40 (1) of the Third Schedule to the Act and Section 38 (1) of the Children Act, 1948, the 'local authorities' for the purposes of Section 1 of the Act are in England and Wales the councils and counties and county boroughs.

7. Paragraph 41 of the Third Schedule applies Section 39 of the Children Act, 1948 (under which various child care functions of a local authority stand referred to their children's committee), to the exercise of a local authority's functions under Part I and Part III (except Section 56) of the present Act. Local authorities' functions under Section 1 accordingly stand referred to their children's committees.

8. Responsibility for ensuring that the advice, guidance and assistance mentioned in sub-section (1) is provided rests on the local authority, but under sub-section (2) it will be open to the local authority to make arrangements for the provision of these services with voluntary organisations or other persons. The reference to 'other persons' allows a local authority to enlist the help of any suitable agency (including another local authority) even if it is not a voluntary organisation.

9. Under sub-section (3) a local authority are not required to provide advice, guidance or assistance which would duplicate facilities already available under another enactment. But the authority may, if they think it desirable, make such separate provision under the section as they consider appropriate for families where the children's welfare is at risk.

10. Under sub-section (4) a local authority are required to make such reports to the Secretary of State as he may specify on the nature of the provisions which have been made by the authority under the section. A report must be furnished at least once in every twelve months.

Appendix 3. Analysis of circumstances of families in the main study

	Group 1		Group 2		Group 3	
Relationship of adults in family unit						
Total sample in main study	65		83		89	
	No.	*%*	*No.*	*%*	*No.*	*%*
Married parents	36	55	48	58	49	55
Cohabiting	4	6	4	5	10	11
One parent	21	32	27	32	25	29
Other	3	5	1	1	2	2
Family disappeared	1	2	3	4	3	3
Total	65	100	83	100	89	100

	Group 1		Group 2		Group 3	
Past care or court appearances						
	No.	*%*	*No.*	*%*	*No.*	*%*
Families having had children in care	31	47	47	57	22	25
No children in care	33	51	34	41	63	71
Not known if in care	1	2	2	2	4	4
Total	65	100	83	100	89	100
Children before court during previous five years	14	22	22	27	11	12

The remainder had no court appearance during this period.

	Group 1		Group 2		Group 3	
Housing						
	No.	*%*	*No.*	*%*	*No.*	*%*
Rented: local authority	54	82	65	79	63	71
privately	7	11	11	13	9	10
Other housing	3	5	6	7	14	16
Homeless	1	2	1	1		
Not known					3	3
Total	65	100	83	100	89	100

	Group 1		Group 2		Group 3	
Length of residence in the area						
	No.	*%*	*No.*	*%*	*No.*	*%*
Over five years	49	75	53	64	49	55
Under five years	15	23	30	36	30	34
Not known	1	2			10	11
Total	65	100	83	100	89	100

Socio-economic grouping

	No.	%	No.	%	No.	%
Unskilled manual	34	52	30	36	22	25
Semi-skilled manual	14	22	18	22	29	33
Skilled manual	6	9	14	17	9	10
Non-manual			10	12	17	19
Other including mother alone and not working	10	15	11	13	10	11
Not known	1	2			2	2
Total	65	100	83	100	89	100

Main current source of income

	No.	%	No.	%	No.	%
Father's earnings	19	29	34	41	50	56
Mother's earnings	1	2	2	2	6	7
Maintenance					3	3
Supplementary or national insurance benefit	41	63	46	56	27	31
Not known	4	6	1	1	3	3
Total	65	100	83	100	89	100

Schoolchildren in family receiving free school meals

	No.	%	No.	%	No.	%
All or some	45	69	47	57	25	29
None	7	11	14	17	34	38
No school children in family	7	11	15	18	10	11
Not known	6	9	7	8	20	22
Total	65	100	83	100	89	100

Debts a problem when case opened

	No.	%	No.	%	No.	%
Yes	49	75	57	69	54	61
No	14	22	14	17	17	19
Not known	2	3	12	14	18	20
Total	65	100	83	100	89	100

Case workers' assessment of success in attaining their case work goals

	No.	%	No.	%	No.	%
Attainment of short-term goals:						
Case successful	60	92	71	86	75	85
Case unsuccessful	5	8	11	13	10	11
No short term goal					3	3
Unable to assess			1	1	1	1
Total	65	100	83	100	89	100

Attainment of long term goals:

Case successful	23	35	19	23	12	14
Case unsuccessful	11	17	17	20	9	10
Insufficient time to judge	29	45	44	53	54	61
No long term goal	2	3	3	4	10	11
Not completed/unable to assess					4	4
Total	65	100	83	100	89	100

A further note on financial circumstances of families in main study

	Group 1		Group 2		Group 3	
	No.	%	*No.*	%	*No.*	%

Income of families measured against current short-term supplementary benefit

Income more than 50p *above* STS rate	18	28	29	36	29	32
Income *on* STS rate	21	32	19	13	12	14
Income more than 50p *below* STS rate	18	28	12	14	8	9
Subsistence rate not assessible			6	7	6	7
Income not known	8	12	17	20	34	38
Total	65	100	83	100	89	100

Income on or below subsistence level

As a percentage of known income	68	47	36
As a percentage of assessible income	68	52	50

In view of the large number of cases where the income was not known, these were examined further in terms of source of income.

In Group 1 in all but Angleshire the families were receiving supplementary benefit, which probably means that the above percentage is an under-estimate of the number of poor families.

In Group 2 in all departments the families where income was not known were evenly divided between those receiving benefit and those earning, thus not radically affecting the above percentage.

In Group 3 in Nordale and Colton, followed by Milltown, the overwhelming majority of cases were reliant upon the father's earnings, with only three cases known to be receiving free school meals, thus reinforcing the picture that this group may be better off financially. However, the uptake of benefits amongst working fathers is known to fall well below entitlement. In Felcastle and the Welsh county the few cases were evenly divided.

The percentages relating to individual departments are given below.

	Group 1	Group 2	Group 3
Income on or below subsistence level as a percentage of known income			
Milltown	71	45	22
Nordale	70	84	33
Welsh county	69	31	31
Colton	56	40	50
Felcastle	80	33	25
As a percentage of assessible income			
Milltown	71	62	25
Nordale	70	84	50
Welsh county	69	33	31
Colton	56	44	59
Felcastle	80	33	25

V